McGraw-Hill Reading
WonderWorks

M000102735

Mc
Graw
Hill
Education

Bothell, WA • Chicago, IL • Columbus, OH • New York, NY

Cover and Title Page: Nathan Love

mheducation.com/prek-12

Send all inquiries to:
McGraw-Hill Education
Two Penn Plaza
New York, New York 10121

ISBN: 978-0-02-129796-2
MHID: 0-02-129796-7

Printed in the United States of America.

10 11 12 13 14 QSX 21 20 19 18 17   D

Program Authors

Douglas Fisher

Jan Hasbrouck

Timothy Shanahan

McGraw Hill Education

Bothell, WA • Chicago, IL • Columbus, OH • New York, NY

EUREKA! I've Got It!

The Big Idea

Week 1 · Meeting a Need   18

Week 2 · Trial and Error   30

Go Digital! www.connected.mcgraw-hill.com

Week 3 · Seeing for Yourself   42

Week 4 · Inventions   54

Week 5 · New Technology   66

1

Unit 2

Taking the Next Step

Go Digital! www.connected.mcgraw-hill.com

Unit 3

Getting from Here to There

The Big Idea

Go Digital! www.connected.mcgraw-hill.com

Unit 4

IT'S UP TO YOU

The Big Idea
How do we decide what's important?

Go Digital! www.connected.mcgraw-hill.com

(t) Jimmy Holder; (b) Elizabeth Buttler

6

Unit 5

What's Next?

The Big Idea

(t) Rogerio Soud; (b) Ron Mazellan

  **Go Digital!** www.connected.mcgraw-hill.com

Linked In

Go Digital! www.connected.mcgraw-hill.com

(t) Lophelia II 2009 Expedition, NOAA-OER; (c) Alfred Eisenstaedt/Time & Life Pictures/Getty Images, (b) Peter Zelei/Vetta/Getty Images

A C T
Access Complex Text

Some text can be hard to understand. It can be complex. But you can figure it out! Take notes as you read. Then ask yourself questions.

Vocabulary

☐ Did I look for context clues to help me figure out words I don't know?

☐ Did I use a dictionary to look up technical terms?

Make Connections

☐ Did I connect ideas from one part of the text to another?

☐ Did I connect two or more details in the text?

Text Features

☐ Are there illustrations or photos that help me understand the text?

☐ Is there a map or a diagram that gives me information?

☐ Did I read all the captions and headings?

Text Structure

☐ Did I look for clues to help me understand how the text is organized?

☐ What kinds of sentences are in the text and what do they tell me?

Text Evidence

The details in the text are the clues that will help you answer a question. These clues are called text evidence. Sometimes you will find answers right there in the text. Sometimes you need to look in different parts of the text.

It's Stated – Right There!

☐ Can I find the answer in one sentence?

☐ Do I need to look for details in more than one place in the text?

☐ Do the words in the text tell the exact answer?

☐ Did I put information from different parts of the text together?

☐ Did I use evidence to answer the question?

It's Not Stated – But Here's My Evidence

☐ Did I look for important clues in the text?

☐ Did I put the clues in my own words?

☐ Did I put the clues together?

☐ Did I use the clues to answer the question?

Talk About It

Talking with your classmates is a great way to share ideas and learn new things. Have a good idea? Share it! Not sure about something? Ask a question!

When I Talk

☐ Did I use complete sentences?

☐ Did I talk about one topic and describe the key details?

☐ Did I answer the question?

☐ Did I speak clearly?

When I Listen

☐ Did I listen carefully when others spoke?

☐ Did I understand the key ideas?

☐ If I didn't understand something, did I ask a question?

☐ Did I ask questions about the topic so I could learn more?

Discussion Rules

☑ Be respectful.

☑ Speak one at a time.

☑ Listen to others with care.

Mike Moran

Write About Reading

A good way to think about what you have read is to write about it. You can write to tell what you think. You can write to share what you learned. Use evidence from the text to support your ideas and opinions.

Getting Ready to Write

☐ Did I look back at my notes about what I read?

☐ Did I find text evidence to support my opinions or ideas?

Writing Opinions

☐ Did I tell my opinion with a topic sentence?

☐ Did I use text evidence to support my opinion?

☐ Did I end with a strong conclusion?

☐ Did I use complete sentences?

Writing Informative Texts

☐ Did I start with a clear topic sentence?

☐ Did I use facts and details from the text to develop my topic?

☐ Did I end with a strong conclusion?

☐ Did I use complete sentences?

EUREKA!

I've Got It!

THE BIG Idea

Where can an idea begin?

Talk About It

Weekly Concept Meeting a Need

Essential Question

How do we get the things we need?

Go Digital!

Write words that describe what the family is doing to meet a need. Then write other ways people can get the things they need.

Food

Water

Meeting Needs

Clothing

Shelter

Describe a time when you got something you needed. Use some words you wrote above.

Vocabulary

 Work with a partner to complete each activity.

1 prosper

The phrase *do well* is a synonym for *prosper*. Circle two words below that are also synonyms for *prosper*.

succeed   grow   fail

2 savings

Write one way you could build your *savings*.

_____

3 afford

Look around the classroom. Write two things you would like to be able to *afford*.

_____

_____

4 loan

Explain why you might ask a friend for a *loan*.

_____

_____

5 risk

List two sports in which players take a big *risk*.

_____

_____

6 profit

Which sentence tells how to make a *profit*?

Make less money than you spend.

Make more money than you spend.

7 scarce

Name something in the classroom that often becomes *scarce*. What do you do when it is *scarce*?

_____

_____

_____

_____

8 wages

Draw a picture of something you can do to earn *wages*.

High-Utility Words

▶ **Sequence Words**

Sequence words are words that tell the order of events.

Circle the sequence words in the passage.

Danny forgot his spelling list at school. (First) Danny called Sam. However, Sam was not home. He was at football practice. Next Danny called Grace, but she was out, too. Finally Danny called Ana. She was home! Ana read the words to Danny. He wrote them down. Then he studied them. The next day, Danny did well on the spelling test.

Use this page to take notes as you read "A Fresh Idea" for the first time.

A Fresh Idea

Essential Question

How do we get the things we need?

Read about how one girl meets a need in her neighborhood.

One bright Saturday morning, Mali and her mom walked around the neighborhood. Mom walked. Mali skipped, jumped over puddles, and then paused to look at the budding trees. "I can't wait until summer," she said. "I love the tomatoes Mrs. Fair sells at her market **stand**." She pointed.

Mali's mom looked at the empty lot. Mrs. Fair set up her stand there every summer weekend. She turned to Mali. "Honey, Mrs. Fair told me last week she had to close her stand. She said she is getting too old to run it."

"The stand can't close!" Mali said. "It's the only place to buy fresh tomatoes." To show she wasn't selfish, she added, "we all need fruits and vegetables."

After they got home, Mali went to her backyard to think. "I wish I could grow tomatoes," she thought. "But our yard is too small." Just then, she noticed her neighbor Mr. Taylor looking at his flowers. She knew he had planted the daffodils with his wife, who had died only a year ago. Mali saw the sadness on his face. Then she had an idea.

Valeria Docampo

Text Evidence

1 Expand Vocabulary

A **stand** is a table or booth at a market. **Circle** the details that are clues to the meaning of the word *stand* in the story.

2 Connection of Ideas A C T

Underline two details that show what Mali thinks about Mrs. Fair's tomatoes. Why does Mali wish she could grow tomatoes?

_____

_____

3 Comprehension
Sequence

Reread the last paragraph. **Draw a box** around the name of the character that Mali sees when she gets back home. What event happens after?

_____

_____

23

Text Evidence

① Connection of Ideas A C T

Reread the first paragraph.
Underline what Mali says she wants.
What is Mali's idea?

_____

_____

_____

② Expand Vocabulary

An **allowance** is money someone,
such as a parent, gives you at regular
times. **Circle** clues to the meaning of
the word *allowance*.

③ Comprehension
Sequence

Write "1" next to the sentence
that tells what happens after Mali
buys tomato plants. **Write "2"** next
to the sentence that tells what
happens next. What steps do Mali
and Mr. Taylor do last?

_____

_____

"Hi, Mr. Taylor," Mali called.
He waved and turned away.
"Wait!" Mali cried. Taking a
risk, she rushed to explain her
idea, but her thoughts came out
all at once: "Mrs. Fair is closing
her tomato stand. She says she's
getting too old. So I want to grow
tomatoes. I want you to keep
your daffodils, though."

Mr. Taylor smiled. "I'm not
sure what you're talking about.
But you've made me smile.
Reasons to smile have been **scarce**
lately. What do you want to do?"

As Mr. Taylor listened, an
idea came to him. "I still want
my flowers, but there's room for
tomatoes. I will make you a **loan**.
You can use some of my land. I'll

help you, and when your garden
starts to **prosper**, you can repay
me with tomatoes."

They shook hands on this
deal. "But first," Mr. Taylor said,
"you'll have to invest in some
tomato plants."

"Well, I have **savings** from my
allowance. I was saving money
to buy a computer game." She
paused. "But I'd rather have
tomatoes. Let's start right away!"

The next day, she bought
all the tomato plants she could
afford. Mr. Taylor taught Mali
how to prepare the soil and place
the plants. After that, Mali put
stakes in the ground to hold the
thin plant stems up. Then all they
could do was water, pull weeds,
and wait.

Valeria Docampo

When the fruit ripened, there were dozens of red tomatoes. "There is no way I can eat all these," Mali thought. On Saturday, she and Mr. Taylor filled several crates with ripe tomatoes. They took them to the market. By the end of the day, they had sold all of them. "I got back the money I invested," said Mali, "and I also made a **profit** of twenty dollars!"

Mr. Taylor said, "Those are also your **wages!** You've **earned** that money."

Mali beamed. "Maybe you could sell some of your flowers, too. We could run a stand together!" Mr. Taylor pictured a colorful flower garden. He was already looking forward to next summer.

Text Evidence

① Comprehension

Sequence

Reread the first paragraph. **Write "1"** next to the first event that happens on Saturday. **Write "2"** next to the second event. What happens by the end of the day?

_____

_____

② Expand Vocabulary

To **earn** means to get money through work. **Circle** words that help you understand the meaning of *earned*.

③ Connection of Ideas

Underline a clue to Mr. Taylor's feelings. How did Mr. Taylor's feelings change from the beginning to the end of the story?

_____

_____

25

Respond to Reading

  Discuss Work with a partner. Read the questions below about "A Fresh Idea." Use the discussion starters to answer the questions. Write the page numbers to show where you found text evidence.

? Questions	Discussion Starters	Text Evidence
1 What does Mali need at the beginning of the story?	▸ At the beginning of the story, Mali finds out… ▸ Mali needs…	Page(s): _____
2 What does Mr. Taylor need at the beginning of the story?	▸ When Mali sees Mr. Taylor, he looks… ▸ Mr. Taylor must need… ▸ I know this because…	Page(s): _____
3 What do Mali and Mr. Taylor do to get what they need?	▸ Mali gets an idea to… ▸ Mr. Taylor offers Mali… ▸ One way they both get what they need is by… ▸ I know this because I read…	Page(s): _____

Write Review your notes about "A Fresh Idea." Then write your answer to the question below. Use text evidence to support your answer.

How did Mali and Mr. Taylor each get something they needed?

_____

_____

_____

_____

_____

_____

_____

_____

_____

_____

Valeria Docampo

Write About Reading

Shared Read

Read an Analysis ▸ **Illustrations** Read Sasha's paragraph about "A Fresh Idea." Sasha analyzed an illustration in the story. She told how the illustration gives important details about characters and events.

Student Model

Topic Sentence

Circle the topic sentence. What is Sasha going to write about?

Evidence

Draw a box around the evidence that Sasha includes. What other details from "A Fresh Idea" would you include?

Concluding Statement

Underline the concluding statement. Why is this sentence a good wrap up?

In "A Fresh Idea," the illustration on page 24 gives important details about the characters and events. The illustration shows Mali and Mr. Taylor in the garden. The picture shows that they are happy. The picture shows the tomato plants. The plants have only a few leaves when they are planted. The picture also shows the stakes that hold the plants up. I see that they are tall and narrow sticks. The illustration on page 24 gives all of these important details about Mali's and Mr. Taylor's work in the garden.

Valeria Docampo

28

Leveled Reader

_____

_____

_____

_____

_____

_____

_____

_____

_____

_____

_____

_____

Topic Sentence

- ☐ Include the title of the text you read.
- ☐ Tell which illustration gives important details.

Evidence

- ☐ Describe the most important details you see in the illustration.
- ☐ Explain what each detail tells you about a character or event.

Concluding Statement

- ☐ Restate how the illustration helped you know about a character or event.

29

Talk About It

Weekly Concept Trial and Error

Essential Question

What can lead us to rethink an idea?

Go Digital!

Tell what went wrong for these campers. Then write words that would help them rethink their next camping trip.

Rethinking Ideas

 Describe a time when you had to rethink the way you did something. What helped you the next time? Use some of the words you wrote above.

Vocabulary

Work with a partner to complete each activity.

1 assemble

Read the synonyms below for *assemble*. Add another synonym to the list.

assemble: gather, get together, _____

_____

2 decipher

Write your name so that it would be hard to *decipher*.

_____

3 navigate

List two ways people *navigate* on land.

_____

_____

4 distracted

Name one kind of sound that can *distract* you while you read.

_____

5 retrace

▶ Underline the base word in *retrace*.

▶ Circle the prefix.

▶ What does *retrace* mean?

_____

6 options

Look around the classroom. Name two *options* for places to hang an art project.

_____

_____

7 accomplish

Tell how you feel when you *accomplish* a goal. Explain your answer.

_____

_____

_____

8 anxious

Draw a picture of how you look when you are *anxious*.

High-Utility Words

▶ **Contractions**

A contraction is a shortened form of two words.

Circle the contractions in the passage.

Rosa and Kim were painting their art project. "I can't wait to show this to the class!" Rosa said.

"We aren't finished yet!" Kim said.

"No, but it shouldn't take long," said Rosa. "Don't you think it looks good?"

"Yes!" Kim agreed. "I haven't seen anything better!"

My Notes

Use this page to take notes during your first read of "Whitewater Adventure."

_____

_____

_____

_____

_____

_____

_____

_____

_____

_____

_____

WHITEWATER ADVENTURE

Essential Question

What can lead us to rethink an idea?

Read about how Nina and her family use trial and error to rethink solutions to a problem.

I don't know about you, but I never pictured my family on a whitewater rafting vacation in Colorado. We had tried rafting several times before with guides. We liked it! I come from a family of athletes, but I sometimes have to work hard because I am not as strong as they are. My sister, Marta, is fourteen. Marta thinks it's her mission in life to make sure I do everything perfectly. "Nina, hold your paddle this way," she corrects. Honestly, sometimes she's full of herself. But I guess she means well.

That morning, Dad had us **assemble** our equipment. He then went through his checklist. Only Dad could read his checklist. His handwriting is hard to **decipher**. "Paddles– check. Helmets – check. Life jackets – check. Buckets – check." Then we got in our raft for our second solo trip and headed down the Colorado River.

Mom had mapped out our **route**. It had enough whitewater along the way to make it exciting. It felt great to **navigate** the raft together. Dad and I sat in the back of the raft and guided it. Mom and Marta sat in the front. From time to time, waves slapped against the raft and sprayed water in our faces.

James Bernardin

Text Evidence

❶ Comprehension
Problem and Solution

Who is telling the story? **Circle** the narrator's name. What problem does the narrator face when rafting with her family?

_____

_____

❷ Organization

Reread the first two paragraphs. **Draw a box** around the words that tell you when the family's rafting trip begins. What happened before that?

_____

_____

❸ Expand Vocabulary

A **route** is a path. **Underline** another word in the last paragraph that means almost the same as _route_.

Text Evidence

① Expand Vocabulary

When something comes to a **halt**, it stops. **Underline** what caused the raft to come to a *halt*.

② Comprehension
Problem and Solution

Which character tries to solve the problem first? **Circle** the text that tells what this character does. What does the family try to do next?

_____

_____

③ Comprehension
Problem and Solution

The events are told through the narrator's view. **Draw a box** around the text that shows how the narrator feels about the problem. Why does she feel this way?

_____

_____

_____

Suddenly, I was **distracted** by a bear coming out of the trees. I stopped paddling and just watched it, but it turned and began to **retrace** its steps. Everyone must have been distracted by that bear because we quickly ran into a problem! Our raft came to a **halt**. It didn't move at all.

"What's wrong?" I asked, beginning to feel **anxious**.

"Yikes!" said Mom. "We're stuck on some rocks!"

"Maybe a guide will come by and give us a shove," said Marta. But there wasn't a person in sight. She tried shouting for help, "HELLO, OUT THERE!" All we heard back was an echo. To make matters worse, storm clouds were gathering.

"Don't worry," said Dad. "It's the front that's stuck, so let's all sit in the back to shift the raft off the rocks." Carefully, Mom and Marta moved to the rear. Nothing happened.

James Bernardin

"Let's sway from side to side," urged Mom, looking up at the darkening sky. We swayed and swayed, but the raft didn't move an inch. Dad jumped a couple of times, but that didn't work either. Now it started to drizzle. Although no one wanted to **admit** it, we were running out of **options**.

"Wait!" I yelled. I thought back to our rafting lessons. "What if we lift the side of the raft away from the rocks?" I asked hesitantly.

"Quick, let's try it!" said Mom. We lifted the front side away from the rocks. We heard a popping noise.

"Did we tear the raft?" cried Marta.

"No, we broke the suction between the raft and the rocks!" said Dad, pushing off the rocks with his paddle.

"We did it!" yelled Marta. "Nina, that was brilliant!"

"Good thinking, Nina!" cheered Mom and Dad.

By this time, it was raining steadily, so we paddled really hard to return to land and wait indoors for the rain to stop. And how was I feeling? I was on cloud nine! I felt like I could **accomplish** anything I wanted.

Text Evidence

❶ Expand Vocabulary

To **admit** means to agree that something is true. **Underline** the text that tells what the family doesn't want to *admit*.

❷ Comprehension
Problem and Solution

Which character came up with the idea that solved the problem? **Circle** the sentence that describe the idea.

_____

❸ Organization

Draw a box around the sentences that show how the narrator feels at the end of the story. Compare her feelings at the beginning and end of the story. How did her feelings change?

_____

_____

_____

 **Discuss** Work with a partner. Read the questions below about "Whitewater Adventure." Use the discussion starters to answer the questions. Write page numbers where you found text evidence.

? Questions	Discussion Starters	Text Evidence
1 How does Dad think the family can move the raft off the rock?	▶ Dad thinks they can move the raft by… ▶ When the family does this… ▶ I know this because I read…	Page(s): _____
2 What does Mom think the family should do?	▶ Mom thinks the family should… ▶ When the family does this… ▶ I know this because I read…	Page(s): _____
3 What happens when the family tries the narrator's idea?	▶ Nina, the narrator, thinks that they should… ▶ When the family tries her idea… ▶ I know this because I read…	Page(s): _____

Write ▸ Review your notes about "Whitewater Adventure." Then write your answer to the question below. Use text evidence to support your answer.

Why did the family have to rethink ways to move the raft?

_____

_____

_____

_____

_____

_____

_____

_____

_____

_____

James Bernardin

Write About Reading

Shared Read

Read an Analysis **Genre** Read Andre's paragraph about "Whitewater Adventure." Andre tells his opinion about how well the author creates a feeling of suspense.

Student Model

Topic Sentence

Circle the topic sentence. What is Andre going to write about?

Evidence

Draw a box around the evidence that Andre includes. What other details from "Whitewater Adventure" would you include?

Concluding Statement

Underline the concluding statement. Why is this sentence a good wrap up?

I think the author did a good job of creating suspense in "Whitewater Adventure." When the raft stops moving, Nina is anxious. The author doesn't tell why the raft stopped moving right away. This makes me wonder what happened. The author also includes weather details. Storm clouds gather. It starts to drizzle. This adds suspense, too. It makes me wonder if the family will get caught in a storm. All of these details show that the author did a good job of creating suspense.

Leveled Reader

Write an Analysis ▸ Genre Write a paragraph about "Dog Gone." Tell your opinion about how well the author creates a feeling of suspense.

_____

_____

_____

_____

_____

_____

_____

_____

_____

_____

_____

_____

_____

_____

Topic Sentence

☐ Include the title of the text you read.

☐ Tell your opinion about how well the author creates suspense.

Evidence

☐ Include details that create suspense.

☐ Tell why these details made you wonder what would happen next.

Concluding Statement

☐ Restate your opinion.

☐ Tell how all of the details you chose support your opinion.

Talk About It

Essential Question

How can experiencing nature change the way you think about it?

Go Digital!

42

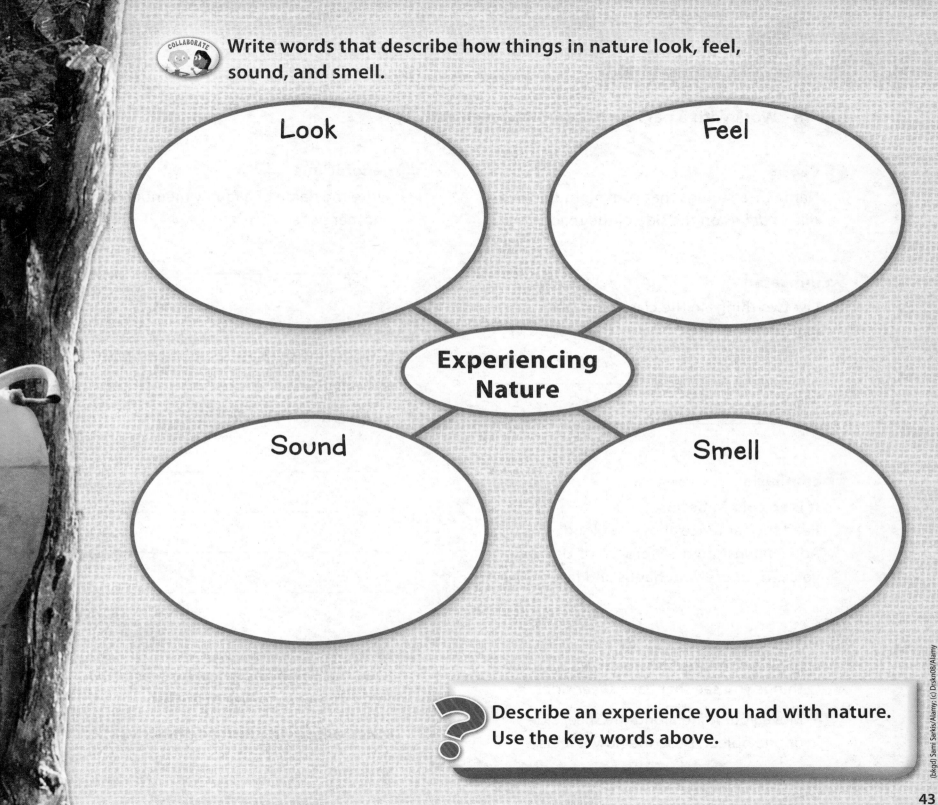

Write words that describe how things in nature look, feel, sound, and smell.

Look

Feel

Experiencing Nature

Sound

Smell

Describe an experience you had with nature. Use the key words above.

Vocabulary

 Work with a partner to complete each activity.

1 debris

Name three things that you might find in a pile of *debris* on the side of the road.

2 indicated

List two things in the classroom that *indicate* time.

_____

_____

3 emphasis

It is so cold in here!
Read the sentence above out loud.
Add *emphasis* to the word "cold." Use your voice. Then use your hands and face.

4 sheer

▶ Look around the classroom. Name three things you see that have *sheer* sides.

▶ Move your hand along the *sheer* side of one object. Describe how it feels.

5 generations

Write the name of a family member from another *generation*.

_____

6 naturalist

▶ Underline the base word in *naturalist*.

▶ Circle the suffix.

▶ What does *naturalist* mean?

_____

_____

_____

_____

7 spectacular

Read the synonyms below for *spectacular*. Add another synonym to the list.

spectacular: wonderful, impressive,

amazing, _____

44

8 encounter

Draw a picture of something you might have an *encounter* with on the beach.

High-Utility Words

▶ **Prepositions**

Prepositions are words that show a direction or a location of something.

Circle the prepositions in the passage.

Tom lived (in) the top apartment of a big house. In his bedroom, books were stacked against the wall. His friend Jeff lived in the apartment under his. Tom and Jeff walked up and down the stairs and visited each other. They went to the park and looked at the tall trees. They also walked around the lake with Tom's dog. They loved their neighborhood!

My Notes

Use this page to take notes during your first read of "A Life in the Woods."

A Life in the Woods

Essential Question

How can experiencing nature change the way you think about it?

Read about how Thoreau's stay in the woods changed his view of nature.

Into the Woods

Henry David Thoreau raised his pen to write. Then the chatter of guests in the next room filled his ears. He **stared** at the page. So far, he had only written, "Concord, MA, 1841." How could he write a book? There was so much noise in his family's house. So Thoreau headed outside. He shut the front door hard with **emphasis** because he was upset. He knew one thing. He had to find a place of his own.

Thoreau walked out of town and into the woods. He liked the sound of the rustling leaves. "I could stay here," he thought. He could live close to nature and begin his book. It would take work, but he could do it.

A friend helped Thoreau get a place in the woods. The friend had land near Walden Pond. He let Thoreau use the land. In March, 1845, Thoreau began to build a cabin there. By July, it was ready. So now Thoreau could live in the woods and write.

Text Evidence

❶ Expand Vocabulary

Stared means to have looked at something for a long time. What did Thoreau *stare* at? Why did he *stare*?

_____

_____

_____

❷ Sentence Structure Ⓐ Ⓒ Ⓣ

The quotation marks " " mean someone is speaking or writing. Reread the first paragraph. **Draw a box** around the text in quotation marks. Who is speaking or writing?

_____

_____

❸ Comprehension
Cause and Effect

Reread the page. **Circle** each cause. **Underline** each effect.

1 Expand Vocabulary

A **habit** is the way an animal behaves. **Draw a box** around the details that tell about the *habits* of a loon.

2 Sentence Structure

What feeling does the author express about where the loon came up? What clue tells you how the author feels?

_____

_____

_____

_____

3 Comprehension
Cause and Effect

Reread the page. **Circle** each cause. **Underline** each effect.

Cabin Life

Thoreau's move to the woods **indicated**, or showed, that he liked to be alone. But Thoreau did not feel alone. Red squirrels ran up and down the **sheer**, steep sides of his cabin. A snowshoe hare lived in a pile of **debris** under the house. Thoreau wrote about these experiences. Writing was easy because this place was so beautiful! And he had much to write about.

On Walden Pond

Thoreau was a **naturalist**. He studied nature and noticed the **habits** of animals. Every time he met an animal, he learned something new. During one **encounter**, Thoreau watched a loon. The bird dove quickly into the pond. Then it swam under the water. Thoreau guessed where it would come up. He was wrong. The loon came up somewhere else! Each time, the loon let out a call. It sounded like a howling laugh. Thoreau felt as if the bird was laughing at him. He wrote in his journal:

At length he uttered one of those prolonged howls, as if calling on the god of the loons to aid him, and immediately there came a wind from the east and rippled the surface, and filled the whole air with misty rain, and I was impressed.

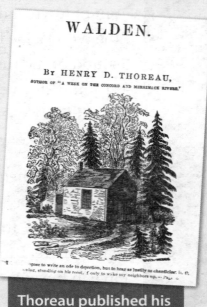

Thoreau published his book *Walden* in 1854.

Loons are still a common sight on Walden Pond.

It was a **spectacular** scene. Thoreau was amazed by the loon's beauty. It no longer seemed like a silly animal. It now seemed to have some strange power.

As months went by, Thoreau saw each animal's ability to stay alive. In winter, he warmed his cabin by fire and watched the moles outside in **awe**. They warmed their nest with their own body heat. Because Thoreau watched the animals, he understood forest life better.

Back to Concord

Like the geese, Thoreau left Walden Pond at the season's end. He had done what he had set out to do. He had learned much from the woods. So he packed his stack of journals and returned to Concord. Now, he would use his journals to write a book called *Walden*. Future Americans would read it. And **generations** to come would discover life on Walden Pond!

Text Evidence

1 Expand Vocabulary

When you are in **awe**, you are amazed by something. **Draw a box** around the sentence that tells why Thoreau watched the moles in *awe*.

2 Sentence Structure

Reread the first sentence in the last paragraph. What does the author compare? How are they alike?

_____

_____

_____

3 Comprehension
Cause and Effect

Reread the page. **Circle** each cause. **Underline** each effect. What caused Thoreau to write the book *Walden*?

_____

_____

Respond to Reading

 COLLABORATE

 **Discuss** Work with a partner. Use the discussion starters to answer the questions below about "A Life in the Woods." Write the page numbers where you found text evidence.

? Questions	**Discussion Starters**	**Text Evidence**
1 What did Thoreau think about nature at first?	▶ Before he moved to the woods, Thoreau thought… ▶ Thoreau's first thoughts about nature were… ▶ I know this because I read ….	Page(s): _____
2 What did Thoreau think about nature after living in the woods?	▶ After living in the woods, Thoreau thought… ▶ I know this because I read…	Page(s): _____
3 What caused Thoreau to change the way he thought about nature?	▶ One thing that caused Thoreau to change the way he thought about nature was… ▶ Another reason Thoreau's thoughts about nature changed is because …. ▶ I noticed that…	Page(s): _____

Write Review your notes about "A Life in the Woods." Then write your answer to the question below. Use text evidence to support your answer.

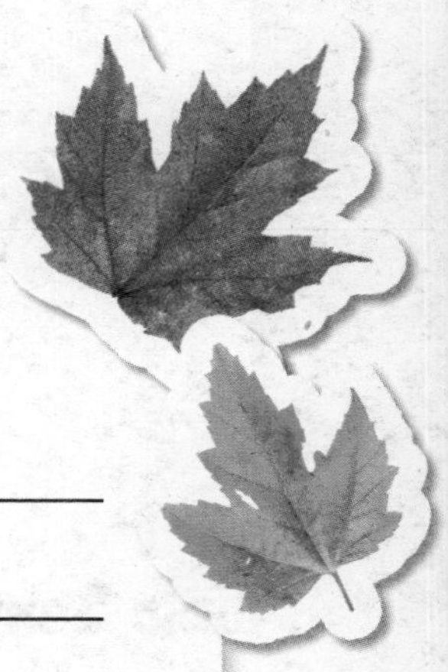

How did the things Thoreau saw change the way he thought about nature?

D. Hurst/Alamy

Write About Reading

Read an Analysis **Genre** **Read David's paragraph below about "A Life in the Woods." He wrote about how the author uses Thoreau's own words to support an idea.**

Student Model

Topic Sentence

Circle the topic sentence. What information does David include in this sentence?

Evidence

Draw a box around the evidence David includes. What other information from "A Life in the Woods" would you include?

Concluding Statement

Underline the concluding statement. Why is the sentence a good wrap up?

> In "A Life in the Woods," the author uses Thoreau's own words to show that Thoreau changed. Thoreau went to live in the woods. He watched animals there. The author includes Thoreau's writing. It tells about a loon Thoreau watched on the pond. This writing also tells what Thoreau was thinking. He thought the animal was silly at first. Thoreau wrote that the loon impressed him. The author's use of Thoreau's own words helped me understand that Thoreau's view of nature changed.

Leveled Reader

Write an Analysis **Genre** Write a paragraph about "Save This Space!" Tell how the author uses Aldo Leopold's own words to support the idea that Leopold changed.

_____

_____

_____

_____

_____

_____

_____

_____

_____

_____

_____

Topic Sentence

☐ Include the title of the text.

☐ Tell the author's main idea. State that the author's use of Leopold's words supports this idea.

Evidence

☐ Include Leopold's words that the author used in the text.

☐ Explain why these words support the author's idea.

Concluding Statement

☐ Restate that the author's use of Leopold's words support the main idea.

Talk About It

Weekly Concept Inventions

Essential Question

How does technology lead to creative ideas?

Go Digital!

54

Name the inventions you see in the photograph. Write words to describe what these inventions help the girl do.

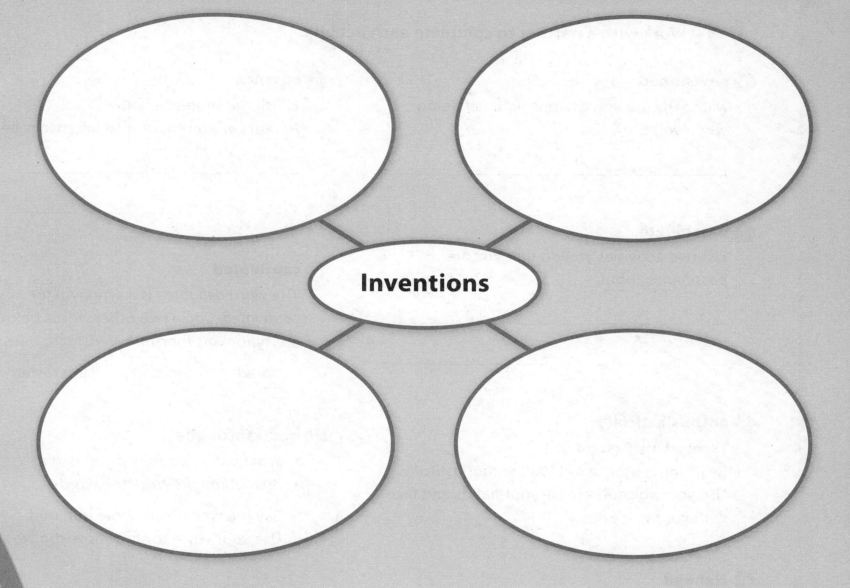

Inventions

Tell your favorite technology. What does this invention help you do? Use some of the words you wrote above.

Vocabulary

 Work with a partner to complete each activity.

1 envisioned

Name the job you *envision* yourself doing when you grow up.

_____

2 passionate

List two activities you do that you are *passionate* about.

_____

_____

3 enthusiastically

I scored my first goal!

Read the sentence out loud *enthusiastically*. Use your voice. Then use your hands and face with your voice.

4 claimed

Name something in the classroom that you have *claimed*.

_____

5 patents

Finish the sentence below.
***Patents* are important to inventors because**

_____

_____

6 captivated

The word *delighted* is a synonym for *captivated*. Circle two other words below that are synonyms for *captivated*.

bored   amazed   interested

7 breakthrough

▶ What would you say if you had a *breakthrough*? Write the words.

▶ Say the words you wrote out loud. Use your voice to show how you would feel.

_____

_____

8 **devices**

Draw a picture of a *device* you use every day.

High-Utility Words

▶ Linking Words

Linking words are used to connect or join ideas.

Circle the linking words in the passage.

Meg is very smart (and) likes to make things. Meg wanted to make a costume for her sister Gabby. "Would you like to be a lion or a princess?" Meg asked. Gabby wanted to be a princess. Meg found scraps of cloth but only had pins to attach them. Mom got her a needle and thread. Meg sewed the cloth together and made a dress. Gabby put it on and showed Mom her new costume.

My Notes

Use this page to take notes during your first read of "Fantasy Becomes Fact."

Fantasy
Becomes Fact

Essential Question

How does technology lead to creative ideas?

Read about how a science fiction writer's ideas led to new technology.

Inventing the Future

Have you ever imagined ways to travel into space? Or used a tool and wished it did something more? Science fiction writer Arthur C. Clarke thought this way. Some of the things he imagined and wrote about became real inventions!

In his writings, Arthur **envisioned** technologies that had not yet been invented. This was no accident. Arthur studied science his whole life. Arthur wrote about advanced computers. He also wrote about spaceships. Years later, these technologies were **developed**.

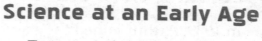

Science at an Early Age

Even as a child, Arthur was **passionate** about science. He was born in England in 1917. He spent his school years **enthusiastically** reading his favorite science fiction magazine. He became fascinated by astronomy. He built a telescope when he was just 13. He also started writing science fiction stories. He published them in a school magazine. Arthur loved imagining the future.

When Arthur was a teenager, his father died. His mother did not have the money to send him to college. So Arthur moved to London. He was 19 years old. He got an office job. But he continued to write science fiction. His love of science would soon be useful.

Arthur C. Clarke sometimes made his own tools for his research.

Text Evidence

1 Connection of Ideas A C T

Reread the second paragraph. **Draw a box** around the details that tell what Arthur wrote about. What do these details tell about Arthur?

_____

_____

2 Expand Vocabulary

When something is **developed**, it is made or created. **Circle** a word in the second paragraph that means the same as _developed_.

3 Comprehension
Sequence

Underline phrases that show the order of events in Arthur's early life. What key events happened before Arthur was 19 years old?

_____

_____

_____

59

Text Evidence

① Connection of Ideas ⒶⒸⓉ

Draw a box around the sentences that describe the wireless system Arthur imagined. What two technologies did Arthur build on to help him come up with his system?

_____

_____

② Expand Vocabulary

If something **exists**, it is real. **Circle** the technology that did not _exist_ when Arthur imagined a wireless communications system.

③ Comprehension
Sequence

Underline the sentence that tells when a satellite communications system was created. What technology became possible later?

_____

_____

Predicting the Future

In 1939, Arthur joined the Royal Air Force. He fought in the Second World War. He also began to invent. Arthur learned to use radar to guide planes. Radar sends and receives radio signals to track objects. This technology gave him ideas. He imagined a **breakthrough** in communication systems. He pictured a wireless system. It would use satellites. Rockets would carry satellites into space. The satellites would send signals around the Earth. Satellites did not **exist** at the time. Arthur used his imagination. He used what he knew about radar and space.

Arthur was like other inventors. He built on technologies that already existed. For example, rockets did exist. But they could not travel into space. In 1957, Russia used a rocket to launch the first satellite into space. It was called Sputnik 1. In the 1960s, a satellite communications system was created. It was like the one Arthur had imagined years before. Years later, the same idea was used to make cell phone communication possible. Arthur **claimed** the communications system as his own idea. He did not, however, apply for **patents**. A patent is a legal claim. As a result, he never made money from his idea.

Satellites like this one began with _Sputnik 1_. It weighed less than 200 pounds. It was only about 23 inches across.

Can Science Fiction Come True?

In 1968, Arthur published *2001: A Space Odyssey.* It is a famous novel about a computer that controls almost everything. The computer's name is HAL. It can think for itself. Today, computers cannot think. However, they do control many **devices**. They control devices in our homes, cars, planes, and spacecraft. In the story, HAL recognizes human voices. It also speaks. This technology did not exist at the time the book was written. But it is **common** today in many computers and cell phones. Arthur's novel also predicted space stations and

Inventors start out by imagining what the future might look like.

missions to far-off planets. In the novel, people even read news on electronic screens!

Arthur C. Clarke's books have **captivated** and delighted readers around the world. Many of the things he wrote about seemed like fantasy at the time. But they turned into fact. His creative ideas may have inspired others to invent the very technologies he imagined.

Text Evidence

❶ Connection of Ideas Ⓐ Ⓒ Ⓣ

Draw a box around details that tell what HAL can do. **Underline** details that tell what computers can do today. How are computers today like HAL? How is HAL different?

_____

_____

_____

❷ Expand Vocabulary

When something is **common**, it is well-known or used by many people. **Circle** a clue to the meaning of the word *common.*

❸ Connection of Ideas Ⓐ Ⓒ Ⓣ

Reread the page. List two technologies Arthur included in his novel that became real inventions.

_____

_____

61

Respond to Reading

 **Discuss** Work with a partner. Use the discussion starters to answer the questions below about "Fantasy Becomes Fact." Write the page numbers to show where you found text evidence.

❓ Questions	 Discussion Starters	🔍 Text Evidence
1 What technology did Arthur learn to use in the Royal Air Force?	▶ While in the Royal Air Force, Arthur learned to use… ▶ I read that this technology was able to…	Page(s): _____
2 What other technology existed when Arthur thought of a communications system?	▶ Another technology that existed when Arthur thought of a communications system was… ▶ I know this because I read that…	Page(s): _____
3 How was Arthur's idea for a communications system different than existing technology?	▶ One way Arthur's idea was different than existing technology was that… ▶ Arthur's idea was also different because… ▶ I read that…	Page(s): _____

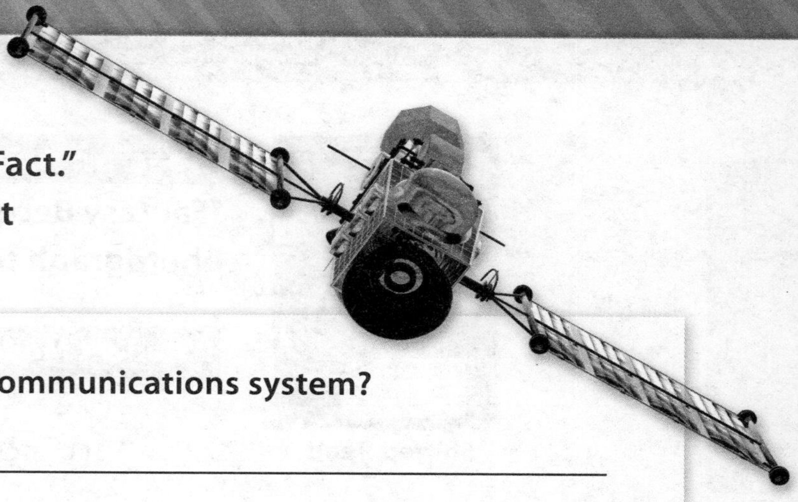

Write Review your notes about "Fantasy Becomes Fact." Then write your answer to the question below. Use text evidence to support your answer.

How did technology help Arthur C. Clarke imagine a new communications system?

Utah Images/NASA/Alamy

Write About Reading

Shared Read

Read an Analysis **Genre** Read Ian's paragraph about "Fantasy Becomes Fact." Ian tells how the author uses a photograph to give important details about Arthur C. Clarke.

Topic Sentence

Circle the topic sentence. What is Ian going to write about?

Evidence

Draw a box around the evidence that Ian includes. What other information from "Fantasy Becomes Fact" would you include?

Concluding Statement

Underline the concluding statement. Why is this sentence a good wrap up?

Student Model

In "Fantasy Becomes Fact," the author uses a photograph to give important details about Arthur C. Clarke. The photograph on page 59 shows Arthur with a tool he made. I can see that Arthur is looking down at the tool and holding it. He looks serious about his work. The tool shown also looks like it has many parts. I can see wires and a tube or lens. This tells me Arthur must be good at putting things together. The photograph the author used tells me a lot about Arthur and his work.

Leveled Reader

_____

_____

_____

_____

_____

_____

_____

_____

_____

_____

_____

_____

Topic Sentence

☐ Include the title of the text.

☐ Tell how the author uses a photograph to give important details about an invention.

Evidence

☐ Tell the page number of the photograph.

☐ Describe the details you see in the photograph.

☐ Explain why these details are important.

Concluding Statement

☐ Restate how the author's use of the photograph helped you know more about the invention.

Talk About It

Essential Question

What are the positive and negative effects of new technology?

Go Digital!

66

Write words that describe the effects of new technology.

Positive
Effects

Positive
Effects

New
Technology

Negative
Effects

Negative
Effects

Tell about a new technology you use.
Describe the effects of using the technology.
Use some of the words you wrote above.

Vocabulary

 Work with a partner to complete each activity.

1 advance

The phrase *go forward* is a synonym for *advance*. Circle another synonym for *advance*.

move ahead   remove   go back

2 data

Which are examples of *data*?

My dog weighs 12 pounds.

I like dogs.

The dog's tail is 4 inches long.

3 access

Name something you need to *access* a locker.

_____

_____

4 cite

Which source would you *cite* for a report on the President?

a biography   an advertisement

5 counterpoint

Write a sentence that is a *counterpoint* to the sentence below.

The movie was exciting.

_____

_____

6 reasoning

Put a check next to two activities that require *reasoning* skills.

_____ solving a jigsaw puzzle

_____ taking a nap

_____ fixing a bicycle

7 drawbacks

What is one *drawback* of staying up late?

_____

_____

_____

68

8 **analysis**

Draw a picture of a tool used to make an *analysis* of an object.

High-Utility Words

▶ **Suffix** *-er*

The suffix *-er* **can mean "one who." For example,** *writer* **means "one who writes."**

Circle words that end with the suffix *-er*.

　　Music class is fun. Our (teacher) Mr. Harper, lets us play different instruments. We play music by famous composers. Each day, one of us gets to be the band leader. I like to be a trumpet player. My best friend Maria likes to be a singer. Mr. Harper says that no matter what we do, we all have to be good listeners. He says it will help us be great performers.

My Notes

Use this page to take notes as you read "Are Electronic Devices Good For Us?" for the first time.

_____

_____

_____

_____

_____

_____

_____

_____

_____

_____

_____

_____

_____

? Essential Question

What are the positive and negative effects of new technology?

Read two different viewpoints about how technology affects kids.

Are Electronic Devices Good for Us?

Plugged In

Electronic devices help kids.

Do you use the Web? Do you play video games? Do you use a cell phone? You are not alone. A new study says kids between the ages of 8 and 19 use computers, cell phones, and video games a lot. Many kids use these devices seven and a half hours a day. Some adults try to **advance** the idea that these activities waste kids' time. But studies do not agree. The **data** show that technology can be good for kids.

Critics say kids stare at screens all day. They say kids do not get enough exercise. The facts stand in **counterpoint** to this belief. One study compared kids who use electronic **media** a lot with kids who do not. Heavy media users got more exercise.

The National Institute of Health found that using computers and video games can help kids. Kids learn to switch tasks easily. Video games may help kids focus. Kids also use the Web to **access** information. Learning to use the Web responsibly can improve kids' **reasoning** skills.

Kids should use technology. The jobs of the future depend on kids who are plugged in!

A Source of News for Teens

Most teens used to get news from print and TV. Many now use the Web to get news.

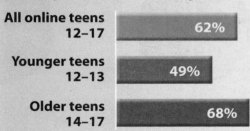

All online teens 12–17	62%
Younger teens 12–13	49%
Older teens 14–17	68%

Text Evidence

1 Expand Vocabulary

Media means tools for communication. **Draw a box** around three examples of *media* in the first paragraph.

2 Comprehension
Author's Point of View

What is the author's position toward kids using electronic devices? **Underline** two details that support this position.

_____

_____

_____

_____

3 Connection of Ideas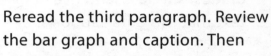

Reread the third paragraph. Review the bar graph and caption. Then **circle** a detail in the text that is supported by information in the bar graph.

71

Text Evidence

1 Comprehension
Author's Point of View

Underline clues to the author's point of view. What is the author's position towards kids using electronic media?

_____

_____

_____

2 Expand Vocabulary

A **report** is the written results of a study. **Draw a box** around the results of a *report*.

3 Connection of Ideas (A)(C)(T)

Which group of media users had the lowest percentage of good grades? **Circle** a sentence in the text that this data supports.

_____

_____

Tuned Out

Electronic media harms kids.

Are electronic devices harmless? Or do they cause problems? One alarming **report** says that young people use electronic devices a lot. Today, they use them an hour more each day than they did 5 years ago. Nearly 7 out of 10 kids have cell phones. An **analysis** of several studies shows this can have disadvantages.

The Web is supposed to be a great tool for learning. But do kids who love computers do better in school? To **cite** one report, more media use does not mean better grades. See the graphs below.

Many young people use more than one device at a time.

Media Use and Grades

Heavy, moderate, and light media users reported their grades. Percentages are rounded.

Heavy Media Users
51% Good grades **47%** Fair/poor grades

Moderate Media Users
65% Good grades **31%** Fair/poor grades

3% School doesn't use grades

Light Media Users
66% Good grades **23%** Fair/poor grades

10% School doesn't use grades

Electronic devices are here to stay. Studying the effects of technology will continue.

Some people claim that using technology helps kids make friends. But the Pew Research Center did a study. It looked at online social networks. Teens stay in touch with friends they already have. They do not use these networks to make new friends. In addition, trying to meet people through the Web can be dangerous.

There are other **drawbacks** to new technology. One issue is that kids do many tasks at once. Can kids do each task well? Some studies say kids' thinking can improve when they multitask. Other experts believe more research is needed.

New electronic devices hit stores every year. Kids should be careful about using too much technology. They must see beyond the screens.

Text Evidence

❶ Comprehension
Author's Point of View

Does the author agree or disagree with the claim that technology helps kids make friends? **Draw boxes** around two facts that support the author's position.

_____

❷ Comprehension
Author's Point of View

Reread the last paragraph. **Underline** a sentence that shows the author's point of view.

❸ Connection of Ideas

Review the first paragraph of each article. **Circle** what the author's agree on. How are the authors' ideas about technology different?

_____

_____

_____

73

Respond to Reading

 **Discuss** Work with a partner. Use the discussion starters to answer the questions about "Are Electronic Devices Good for Us?" Write the page numbers where you found text evidence.

? Questions	Discussion Starters	Text Evidence
1 What are positive effects of kids using the Web?	▶ Using the Web helps kids… ▶ Another good thing about using the Web is… ▶ I read that…	Page(s): _____
2 What are negative effects of kids using the Web?	▶ Using the Web may not help kids… ▶ One bad thing about using the Web to make friends is that… ▶ I know this because I read that…	Page(s): _____
3 What are the positive and negative effects of using devices to multitask?	▶ Multitasking may help kids… ▶ One bad thing about doing many tasks at once is that… ▶ I noticed that…	Page(s): _____

Write Review your notes about "Are Electronic Devices Good for Us?" Then write your answer to the question below. Use text evidence to support your answer.

What are positive and negative effects of kids using electronic devices?

_____

_____

_____

_____

_____

_____

_____

_____

_____

_____

_____

Write About Reading

Shared Read

Read an Analysis ▸ **Point of View** Read Jayden's paragraph below about one of the articles from "Are Electronic Devices Good For Us?" Jayden tells his opinion about how well the author supported a position.

Topic Sentence

Circle the topic sentence. What is Jayden going to write about?

Evidence

Draw a box around the evidence that Jayden includes. What other information from "Plugged In" would you include?

Concluding Statement

Underline the concluding statement. Why is this sentence a good wrap up?

Student Model

In "Plugged In," I think the author did a good job of supporting the position that electronic devices help kids. The author includes facts from studies. One study showed that heavy media users get more exercise. Another study showed that video games may help kids focus. The author includes a graph that shows that 62% of teens get their news online. These facts and details support the position that electronic devices help kids.

Leveled Reader

Write a paragraph about "What About Robots?" Review Chapter 3. Tell your opinion about how the author supports the position that robots are helpful.

_____

_____

_____

_____

_____

_____

_____

_____

_____

_____

_____

_____

Topic Sentence

☐ Include the title of the text you read.

☐ Tell your opinion. Tell whether the author did a good job supporting his or her position.

Evidence

☐ Include details and facts that support the author's position.

☐ Explain why the author did a good job.

Concluding Statement

☐ Restate your opinion about how the author supported his or her position.

77

Unit 2

Taking the Next Step

The Big Idea

What does it take to put a plan into action?

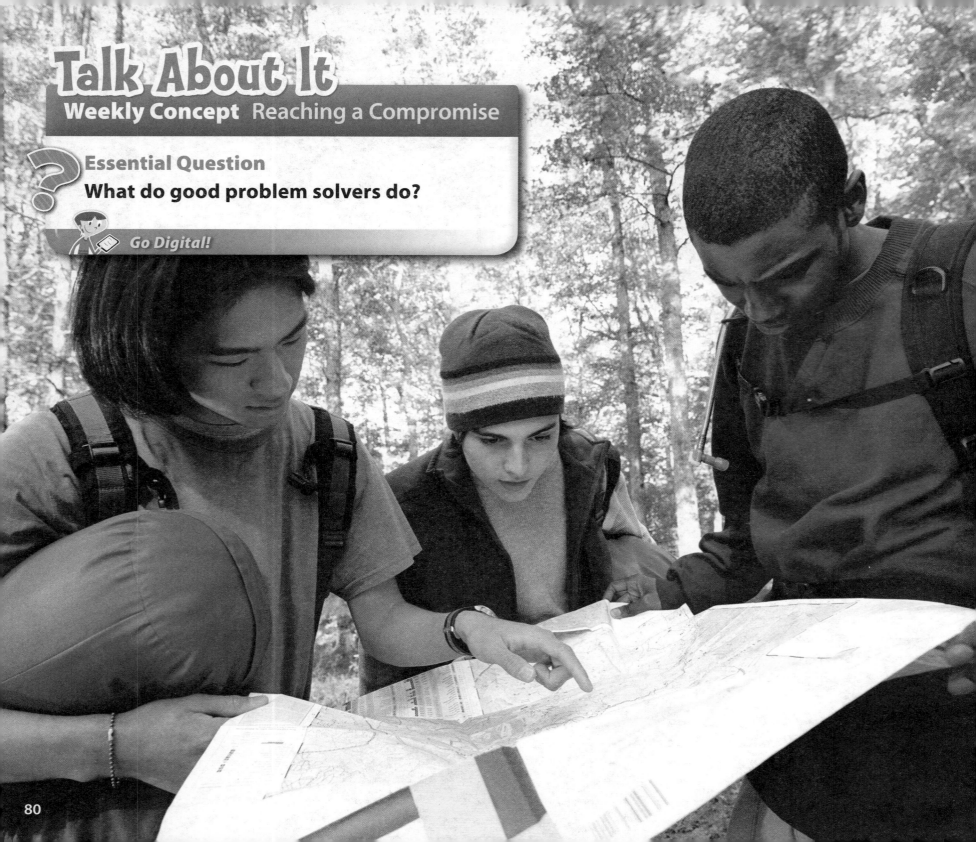

Talk About It

Essential Question

What do good problem solvers do?

Go Digital!

80

Write words that describe different ways a group can solve a problem.

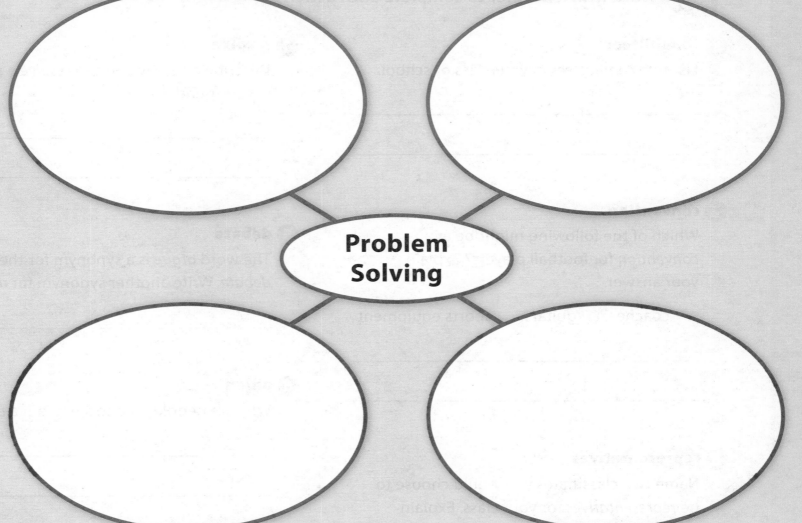

Problem Solving

 Describe a time when you have worked in a group to solve a problem. Use some of the words you wrote above.

Vocabulary

1 committees

List two *committees* in your class or school.

_____

_____

2 convention

Which of the following might be at a *convention* for football players? Explain your answer.

    coaches   guitars   sports equipment

_____

_____

3 representatives

Name two classmates you would choose to be *representatives* for your class. Explain your choices.

_____

_____

4 resolve

Describe one way you can *resolve* a problem with a friend.

_____

_____

5 debate

The word *argue* is a synonym for the word *debate*. Write another synonym for *debate*.

_____

6 union

Why are people on a soccer team a *union*?

_____

_____

7 proposal

Think about ways to improve your school. Tell your partner about a *proposal* you would like to make.

8 situation

Draw a picture to show a *situation* when you wear a helmet.

High-Utility Words

▶ **Time and Sequence Words**

Time and sequence words tell the order of events.

Circle the time and sequence words in the passage.

⟨Last year,⟩ Greendale School had a problem with litter. The principal made a student committee to solve the problem. First, the students put up posters to tell students to clean up. The next day, they watched to see if there was less litter. But after a week, they still found litter around the school. Finally, they decided the school needed more trash cans.

My Notes

Use this page to take notes during your first read of "Creating a Nation."

_____

_____

_____

_____

_____

_____

_____

_____

_____

_____

_____

_____

_____

_____

Creating a Nation

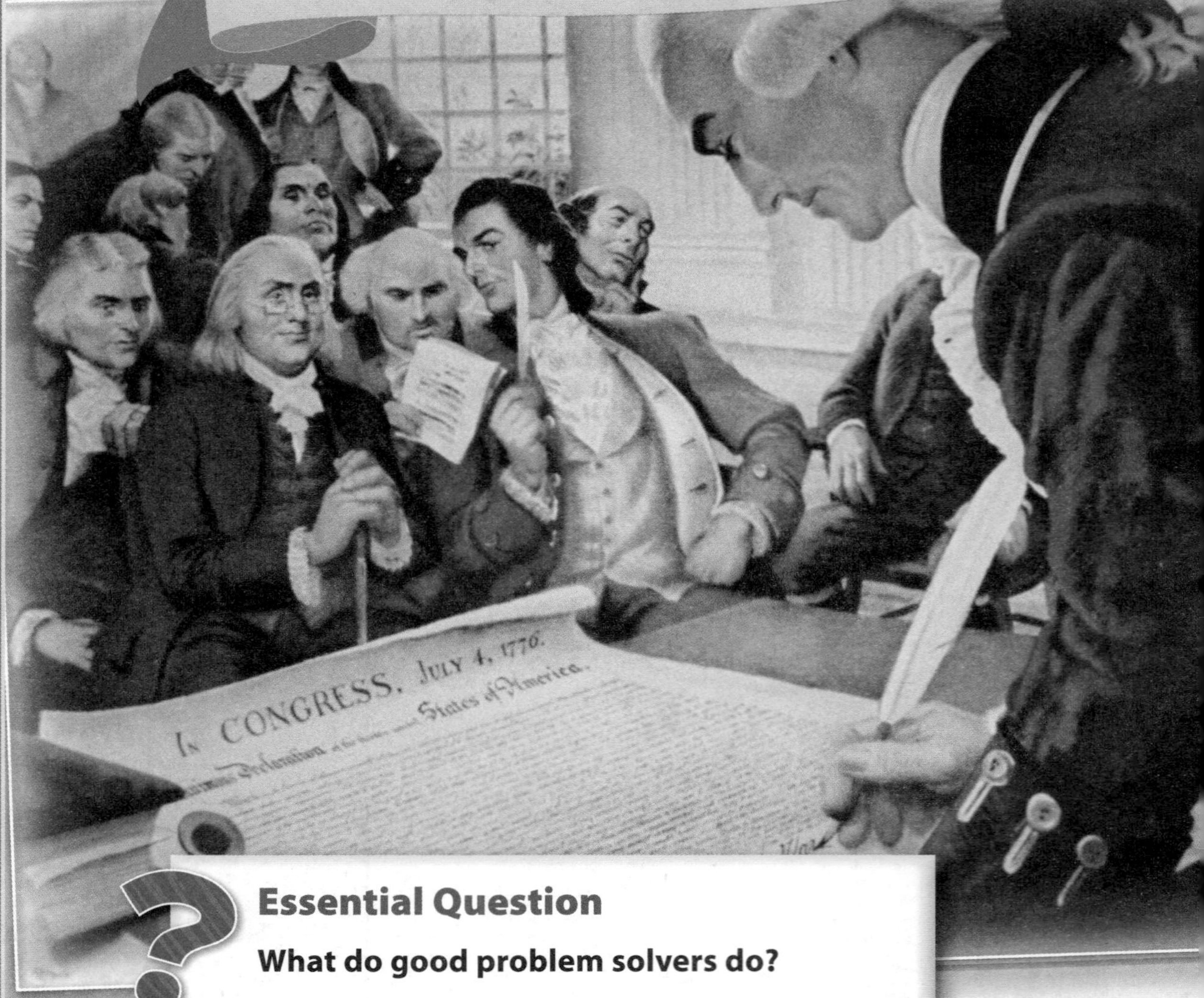

In CONGRESS. JULY 4, 1770.

Essential Question

What do good problem solvers do?

Read about how American colonists tried to solve their problems with Great Britain.

Taxes and Protests

In 1765, King George III of Great Britain needed money to rule his empire. How did he get it? He made colonists pay a tax! The government passed a law called the Stamp Act. Every piece of paper sold in the American colonies had to have a special stamp. Colonists had to pay a tax for the paper.

Most colonists thought the Stamp Act was unfair. British people could choose **representatives** to speak for them in government. Colonists could not do this. So colonists wondered why they had to pay the tax.

Many colonists held **protests**. They wanted to show their dislike for the Stamp Act. Consequently, it was repealed, or canceled. But there were more taxes. There was a tax on cloth that came from Britain. Women protested by weaving their own cloth.

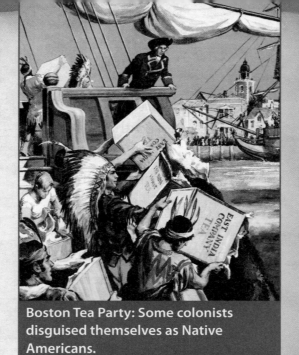

Boston Tea Party: Some colonists disguised themselves as Native Americans.

The **situation** grew worse. In 1770, British soldiers fired into a disorderly crowd in Boston. Five colonists died. This tragedy is known as the Boston Massacre.

By 1773, most taxes had been canceled. However, there was still a tax on tea. Colonists held a protest. One night, they slipped onto British ships in Boston Harbor. They tossed the ships' cargo—tea—overboard. The protest became known as the Boston Tea Party.

Text Evidence

1 Connection of Ideas Ⓐ Ⓒ Ⓣ

Circle text that tells what the Stamp Act forced colonists to do. **Circle** text that tells what British people could do but colonists could not. Why did colonists think the Stamp Act was unfair?

_____

_____

2 Expand Vocabulary

Protests are actions people take to show they are against something. What did women do to *protest* against a tax on cloth?

_____

_____

3 Comprehension
Problem and Solution

Underline the problem colonists faced in 1773. Draw a box around the steps colonists took to solve the problem.

1 Expand Vocabulary

When something is **banned**, it is not allowed. **Circle** what King George *banned*.

2 Comprehension
Problem and Solution

Underline what the patriots wanted to do to resolve problems with the King. **Underline** what the loyalists wanted to do. How did colonists decide what to do?

3 Connection of Ideas

Draw a box around the actions of the First Continental Congress and the Second Continental Congress. How were the actions of each Congress similar and different?

Revolution Begins

King George punished the colonies. He closed the port of Boston. He **banned** town meetings. Colonists called these harsh actions the "Intolerable Acts." However, they couldn't agree on how to **resolve** the problems. Patriots wanted to fight for independence. Loyalists wanted peace with the king. Many colonists were undecided.

Finally, colonists sent representatives from each colony to a **convention** to discuss what to do. This meeting was the First Continental Congress. The delegates decided to send a plan, or **proposal**, for peace to King George. But the trouble continued. In April 1775, British troops began marching to Lexington and Concord. Rumors said they were going to capture weapons that the patriots had hidden there.

The patriots were ready to fight. The British attacked. The patriots fired back. So the British retreated, or moved back.

But war had begun. In May, there was a Second Continental Congress. Delegates made George Washington head of the new army. They also sent another peace proposal to King George.

As the war continued, Congress formed **committees** to do tasks. One committee was chosen to write a declaration of independence. Thomas Jefferson was on this committee. He wrote the document.

Yellow Dog Productions/The Image Bank/Getty Images

Events of the American Revolution

1765	1766	1770	1773	1774
Stamp Act passed		Boston Massacre		First Continental Congress
	Stamp Act repealed		Boston Tea Party	

Independence Declared

Jefferson had to convince many colonists of the need for independence. He used different ideas to persuade them. He said people had rights. These included life, liberty, and the pursuit of happiness. He said King George had taken away colonists' rights. Therefore, the colonies had to separate from Britain.

Congress went on to **debate** and discuss Jefferson's ideas. They removed his strong words against slavery. They made other changes, too. But on July 4, 1776, Congress agreed on and **approved** the Declaration of Independence. A nation was born. Washington's army fought on. In 1778, France joined the fight on America's side. In 1781, British troops surrendered. That same year, Congress approved the Articles of Confederation. The document outlined a government for the new nation. The United States would be a **union** of separate states. The states would have the power to make most decisions.

In 1783, King George finally recognized the nation's independence. However, the new nation's government wasn't working very well. The states often disagreed.

The revolution had ended, but the work of shaping a government had just started. It would continue with a Constitutional Convention in 1787.

1775	1776	1778	1781	1783
• Battle of Lexington and Concord • Second Continental Congress begins	Declaration of Independence	France joins the war	• Last major battle of the war • Articles of Confederation approved	King George recognizes the United States

Text Evidence

① Comprehension
Problem and Solution

According to Jefferson, what problem did King George cause? **Draw a box** around the sentence that tells the problem.

② Expand Vocabulary

To **approve** something means to agree to or accept it. What documents did Congress *approve*?

_____

_____

_____

③ Comprehension
Problem and Solution

Reread the last two paragraphs. **Circle** the sentence that tells the new nation's problem. What was the nation's problem?

_____

_____

Respond to Reading

Discuss Work with a partner. Use the discussion starters to answer the questions below about "Creating a Nation." Write the page numbers to show where you found text evidence.

 **? Questions**

Discussion Starters

 **Text Evidence**

---

1 What did colonists do to solve the problem of the Stamp Act and other taxes?

▶ After the government passed the Stamp Act, colonists...

▶ When there was a tax on cloth from Britain, women...

▶ When there was a tax on tea, colonists...

Page(s): _____

---

2 How did colonists decide what to do to solve the problem of the "Intolerable Acts"?

▶ To decide what to do about the "Intolerable Acts," colonists...

▶ I know this because I read that...

Page(s): _____

---

3 What did Congress do to try to solve problems with Great Britain?

▶ At the First Continental Congress, delegates...

▶ At the Second Continental Congress, delegates...

▶ When the war continued, Congress decided to...

Page(s): _____

Write Review your notes about "Creating a Nation." Then write your answer to the question below. Use text evidence to support your answer.

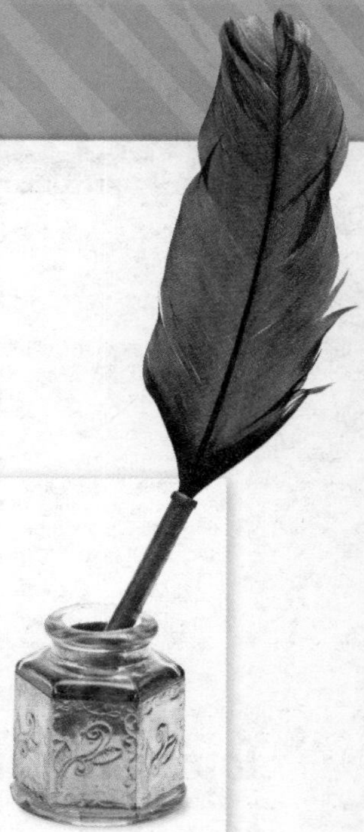

What did the colonists do to try to solve problems with Great Britain?

_____

_____

_____

_____

_____

_____

_____

_____

_____

_____

Write About Reading

Shared Read

Read an Analysis > **Text Structure** Read the paragraph below about "Creating a Nation." Raul analyzed how the author uses headings to organize events.

Student Model

Topic Sentence

Circle the topic sentence. What is Raul going to write about?

Evidence

Draw a box around the evidence that Raul includes. What other information from "Creating a Nation" would you include?

Concluding Statement

Underline the concluding statement. Why is this sentence a good wrap up?

In "Creating a Nation," the author uses headings to organize events that led to the creation of the United States. The first heading is "Taxes and Protests." In this section, the author describes problems in the colonies. The next heading is "Revolution Begins." This part tells about the events that started the war. The last heading is "Independence Declared." This part tells about the events that led to the Declaration of Independence. These headings help me understand the order of events that led to the creation of the United States.

Leveled Reader

Text Structure Write a paragraph about "The Bill of Rights." Review Chapter 3. Write to show how the author uses headings to organize information.

_____

_____

_____

_____

_____

_____

_____

_____

_____

_____

_____

_____

Topic Sentence

☐ Include the title of the text you read.

☐ Tell whether the author uses headings.

☐ Tell whether the headings are connected to the topic of the chapter.

Evidence

☐ Give two or three examples of headings.

☐ Tell how information under each heading is connected to the heading.

Concluding Statement

☐ Restate how the author uses headings to organize information.

Talk About It

Essential Question

What can you do to get the information you need?

Go Digital!

92

Tell how the people in the photograph are getting information. Then write words that describe other ways people can get information.

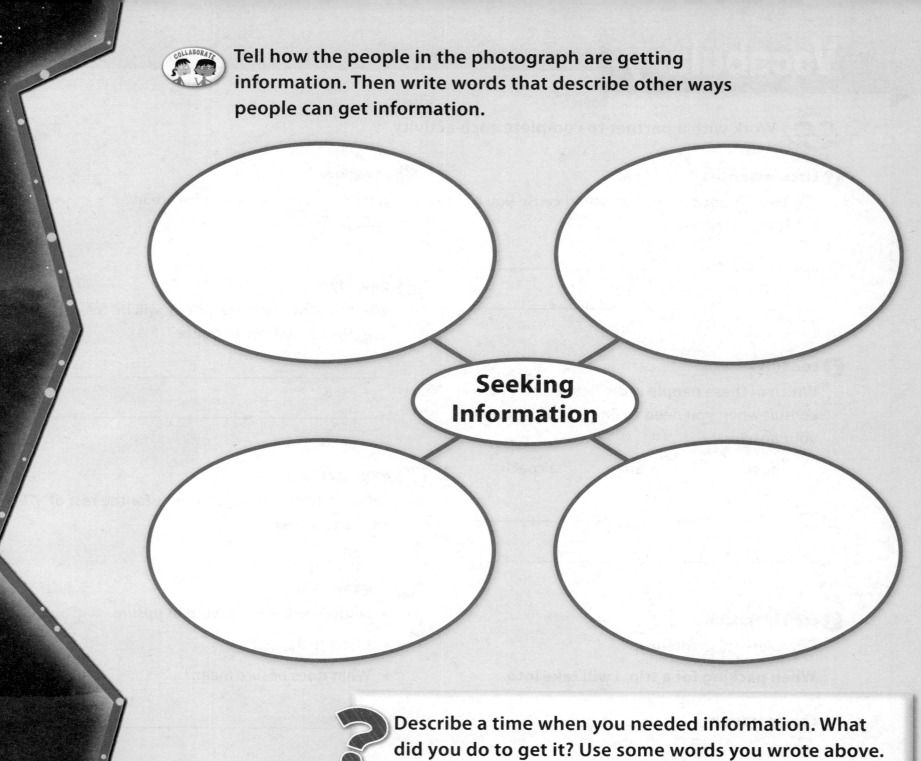

Seeking Information

Describe a time when you needed information. What did you do to get it? Use some words you wrote above.

Vocabulary

 Work with a partner to complete each activity.

1 circumstances

List two *circumstances* that would cause you to close a window.

_____

_____

2 consults

Which of these people is the best person to *consult* when you need to find a book? Explain your answer.

    a doctor   a librarian   a coach

_____

_____

3 consideration

Complete this sentence:

When packing for a trip, I will take into

consideration _____

_____

4 presence

Name three classmates who are in your *presence*.

5 destiny

What do you think the *destiny* will be for someone who likes to dance?

_____

_____

6 expectations

Tell a partner your *expectations* for the rest of the school year.

7 unsure

▶ Underline the base word in *unsure*.

▶ Circle the prefix.

▶ What does *unsure* mean?

_____

_____

8 reveal

Draw something a magician might *reveal* from a hat or box.

High-Utility Words

Contractions

Contractions are two words that are put together. An apostrophe takes the place of some of the letters.

Circle the contractions in the letter.

Dear Anna,

(I'm) writing to tell you about a great fairy tale I read. It's about a princess. She's very strong and brave. She leads a group of people on a quest. They're going to find a dragon. I think you'll agree it's a great story. I'll write soon to find out if you're reading it.

Your friend,
Marcus

My Notes

Use this page to take notes during your first read of "A Modern Cinderella."

_____

_____

_____

_____

_____

_____

_____

_____

_____

_____

_____

_____

A Modern Cinderella

Essential Question

What can you do to get the information you need?

Read how a dancing prince tries to get information about a mystery girl.

Once upon a time—the time being the other night—the Prince was very happy. He had just danced with a young woman at the Royal Palace. It was during the taping of his weekly TV show, *Dancing with the Prince*. He had only agreed to do the show to help his mother, the Queen, raise money for charity. But when the Prince twirled the lovely dancer in the **presence** of the audience, he felt as if he were floating on a cloud.

However, **circumstances** changed at midnight. The young woman's cell phone rang. She rushed from the palace. All she left behind was a purple sneaker.

"I must find her again," the Prince cried. "It must be in time for tomorrow night's final show!" How should he search? He clutched the purple sneaker in his hand.

The Queen saw the Prince's tears. She said, "He who **consults** the right **sources** will succeed." The Prince began thinking. After much **consideration**, he made a plan. First, he talked to everyone who was at the show, but no one could help. Next, the Prince searched the Internet. He entered the phrase "great dancer with purple shoe," but he found no one. Then the Prince put up posters of the purple sneaker all over the kingdom. Yet no one recognized the shoe.

Peter Francis

1 Sentence Structure A C T

Text set between a pair of dashes — — gives more detailed information. **Draw a box** around text between two dashes. What important detail does the author include between the dashes?

_____

2 Expand Vocabulary

People or things that give information are called **sources**. **Circle** the first two *sources* the Prince used to get information.

3 Comprehension
Compare and Contrast

Underline details that show how the Prince felt before midnight. **Underline** details that show how the Prince felt after midnight. How did the Prince's feelings change?

_____

_____

Text Evidence

1 Expand Vocabulary

A **quest** is a search to find something. What does the Prince want to find on his *quest*?

_____

_____

2 Comprehension
Compare and Contrast

Compare events in the third and fourth paragraphs. **Underline** details that show how events are similar. **Circle** details that show how the Prince is different during each event.

3 Sentence Structure Ⓐ Ⓒ Ⓣ

In a story, parentheses ( ) may be set around text that explains a character's actions. **Draw a box** the text in parentheses. What does the text in parentheses explain about the sisters?

_____

_____

_____

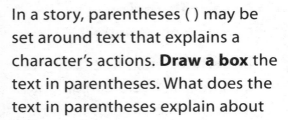

The Prince held the purple sneaker in one hand. "I will continue my **quest**," he cried, "even if I must search the entire kingdom." Then the Prince powered up his electric skateboard and set out!

At the first house, a woman came out to greet the Prince. He held out the sneaker. He said, "This shoe will tell me if you are meant for me. It will tell me my **destiny**." The excited woman struggled to jam her large foot into the shoe, but the sneaker was too small.

At the next house, another woman eagerly tried on the sneaker. The shoe fell off. At every home, the Prince was full of hope, but the purple sneaker was too big or too small. Not one foot met his **expectations**.

The Prince became sad. Finally, there was only one house left. When the Prince arrived, three sisters stood in front, ready to try on the shoe. (They'd been following the news all over the kingdom.) The shoe fit none of them.

"Does anyone else live here?" the tired Prince asked the sisters. From inside the house came a voice. The sisters frowned and their eyes became narrow slits. A young woman stepped outside. She handed her cell phone to the oldest sister.

Peter Francis

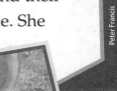

The Prince held out the sneaker. "Please try this on," he **requested**.

She did. It fit her foot perfectly!

"You're my missing dancer!" the Prince cried. "Will you be my dance partner forever?"

The young woman smiled. "Thanks, but not right now. I'll dance tomorrow, but I have a lot of plans. First I want to travel."

The Prince begged, "Please, say yes!"

"Sorry, Prince," the woman said. "You'll just have to wait."

"Okay," the Prince sighed. "But will you **reveal** your name?"

"It's Cinderella." The woman scribbled on a piece of paper. "Here's my number. Let's stay in touch. TTYLP."

The Prince looked **puzzled**. He was **unsure** of how to reply.

"It means Talk To You Later, Prince," Cinderella explained.

"TTYLC," the Prince replied. He waved to Cinderella and rode away.

And they texted happily ever after.

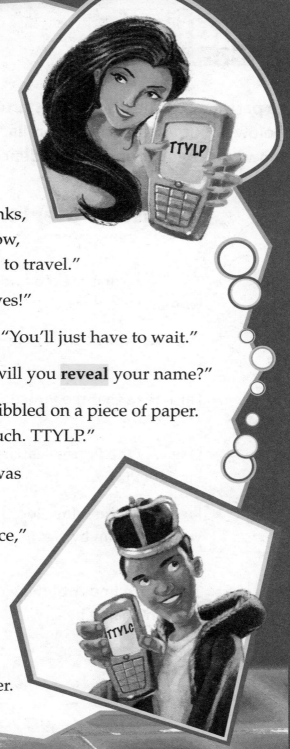

Text Evidence

1 Expand Vocabulary

To **request** means to ask for something. **Circle** the words that tell what the Prince first *requested*.

2 Comprehension
Compare and Contrast

Underline what the Prince hopes the woman will become. **Underline** what the woman plans to do. How are their goals alike and different?

_____

_____

_____

_____

3 Expand Vocabulary

To be **puzzled** is to be confused about something. Why is the Prince *puzzled*?

_____

_____

99

Respond to Reading

Discuss Work with a partner. Use the discussion starters to answer the questions below about "A Modern Cinderella." Write the page numbers to show where you found text evidence.

? Questions	Discussion Starters	Text Evidence
1 At the beginning of the story, what does the Prince do to find the young woman?	▶ The Prince first tries to find the young woman by… ▶ Another way he tries to find her is by… ▶ I also read that the Prince…	Page(s): _____
2 How does the Prince search the kingdom for the young woman?	▶ One way the Prince searches the kingdom is by… ▶ I read that the Prince looks for the young woman by…	Page(s): _____
3 How does the Prince find out the name of the young woman?	▶ The Prince finds out the young woman's name by… ▶ I noticed that…	Page(s): _____

Mike Moran

Write Review your notes about "A Modern Cinderella."
Then write your answer to the question below. Use text
evidence to support your answer.

How does the Prince get the information he needs about the young woman?

_____

_____

_____

_____

_____

_____

_____

_____

_____

_____

_____

Peter Francis

Write About Reading

Shared Read

Student Model

Topic Sentence

Circle the topic sentence. What is Mia going to write about?

Evidence

Draw a box around the evidence that Mia includes. What other details from "A Modern Cinderella" would you include?

Concluding Statement

Underline the concluding statement. Why is this sentence a good wrap up?

In "A Modern Cinderella," the illustrations on the last page give clues to the end of the story. I read that Cinderella wrote her phone number on a piece of paper. She gave it to the Prince. The illustrations show Cinderella and the Prince holding phones. Each phone has a text message. The details in these illustrations are clues that the Prince and Cinderella will send each other text messages.

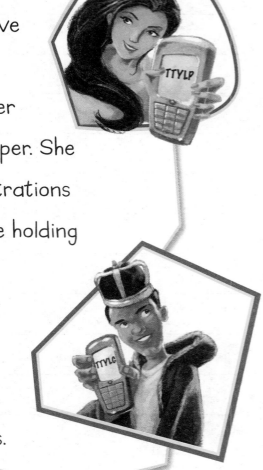

Leveled Reader

Write an Analysis Illustrations **Write a paragraph about "The Bird of Truth." Tell how an illustration in one chapter gives clues to events that happen in another chapter.**

_____

_____

_____

_____

_____

_____

_____

_____

_____

_____

_____

_____

Topic Sentence

☐ Include the title of the text you read.

☐ Tell whether an illustration gives clues to events in another chapter. Include the page number.

Evidence

☐ Describe the illustration.

☐ Tell why details in the illustration are clues to events in another chapter.

☐ Include details from the text.

Concluding Statement

☐ Restate how the illustration gives clues about events in the story.

Talk About It

Weekly Concept Investigations

Essential Question

How do we investigate questions about nature?

Go Digital!

Tell how the people in the photograph are investigating nature. Then write words to describe other ways people investigate nature.

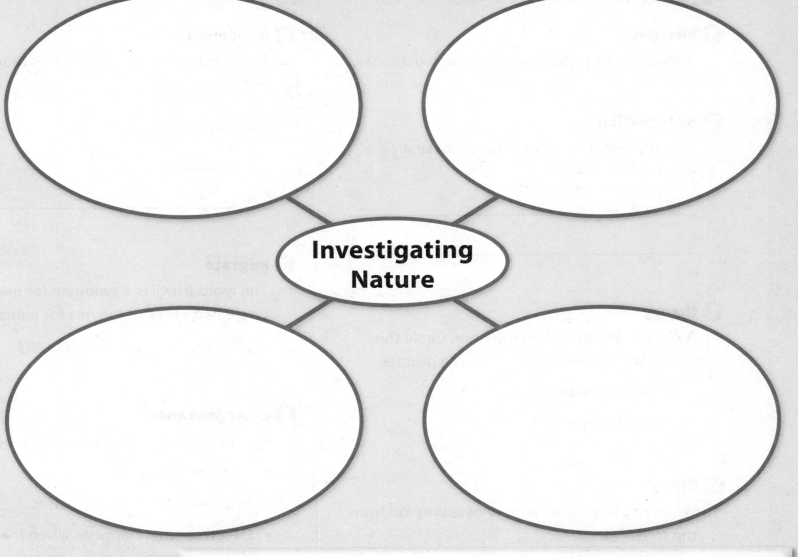

Investigating Nature

 Describe a time when you investigated something in nature. What did you do? Use some of the words you wrote above.

Vocabulary

 Work with a partner to complete each activity.

1 **energetic**

Show how you would walk in an *energetic* way.

2 **observation**

Describe what you would do to make an *observation* about stars.

_____

_____

3 **theory**

A puddle of water is on the floor. Circle the *theory* that explains why there is a puddle.

    A glass of water spilled.

    The lights went out.

4 **flurry**

When might you see a *flurry* of leaves fall from the trees?

_____

_____

5 **behaviors**

List three things you do in class that are good *behaviors*.

_____

_____

_____

6 **migrate**

The word *travel* is a synonym for *migrate*. Circle two other synonyms for *migrate*.

    move   stay   journey

7 **disappearance**

▶ Underline the base word in *disappearance*.

▶ Circle the prefix.

▶ Draw a box around the suffix.

▶ Describe what happens when there is a *disappearance*.

_____

_____

8 transformed

Draw a picture of a plant that needs water. Then draw a picture of how it is *transformed* after someone waters it.

High-Utility Words

▶ **Prepositions**

Prepositions are words that show a direction or a location of something.

Circle the prepositions in the passage.

Katie and Carlos are neighbors. They are planting a garden (between) their houses. First, Katie digs a hole. Then Carlos puts a plant in the hole. Katie presses the soil around the plant. Next Carlos sprays water near the plant's stem. Katie digs another hole by the first plant. Soon they will have a beautiful garden.

My Notes

Use this page to take notes during your first read of "Growing in Place."

_____

_____

_____

_____

_____

_____

_____

_____

_____

_____

_____

_____

_____

Growing in Place

The Story of
E. Lucy Braun

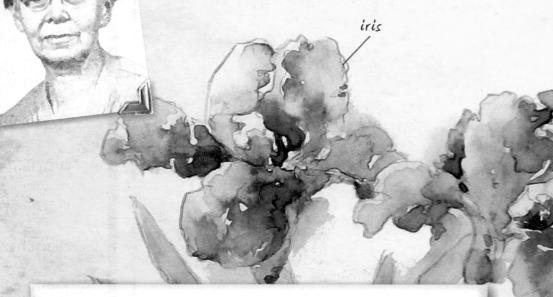

iris

Essential Question

How do we investigate questions about nature?

Read about how Lucy Braun's classification of plants continues to help scientists today.

Lucy's Childhood

Emma Lucy Braun was born in Cincinnati, Ohio, in 1889. She and her mother had the same first name. To avoid confusion, she used her middle name. Her middle name was Lucy. Naming things correctly became the basis for her life's work on plants.

As a child, Lucy was interested in plants. She joined her parents on **energetic** walks through the woods. Her older sister Annette came, too. Lucy enjoyed all the plants and wildflowers.

Lucy asked her mother how to tell the plants apart. Lucy's mother taught her to use her powers of **observation**. She pointed out the number of leaves on a stem. She pointed out the shapes of leaves, too. Lucy wrote notes to keep a **record** of these observations. She also drew what she saw. Then she could see how the plants were alike and different.

Lucy and her mother gathered parts of the plants for their herbarium, a collection of dried plants. They preserved leaves between sheets of paper. They preserved flowers, too. Lucy became more interested in botany. Botany is the study of plants. In high school, Lucy created her own herbarium. She added plants to it all her life.

pink redstem filarees

Text Evidence

1 Purpose (A) C (T)

A biography tells about a person's life. **Circle** the name of the person this biography is about. What was this person interested in?

_____

2 Expand Vocabulary

A **record** is a written description of facts and details. **Draw a box** around the details that Lucy included in her *record* of plants.

3 Comprehension
Sequence

Reread the page. **Write "1"** next to the sentence that tells when Lucy became interested in plants. **Write "2"** next to the sentence that tells when Lucy started her own herbarium.

1 Expand Vocabulary

To **believe** means to think something is true. **Draw a box** around the text that tells what Lucy *believed*.

2 Comprehension

Sequence

Reread the page. **Underline** the year that tells when Lucy began to teach botany. What other subjects did Lucy study before then?

_____

_____

3 Expand Vocabulary

To **tend** means to take care of something. **Circle** clues in the text that help you know the meaning of *tended*. Tell what Lucy *tended*.

_____

_____

Lucy Braun's Snakeroot: This plant grows in Kentucky and Tennessee.

iris

robin's egg

nest

Scientists label sketches to show details.

Lucy Learns More

Later, Lucy went to college. So did Annette. Annette studied insects. Lucy took classes in geology. She studied rocks and minerals. This work **transformed**, or changed, how she looked at nature. She continued her studies in botany as well.

Lucy became interested in ecology. Ecology is the study of how living things behave in their natural settings. Lucy had a **theory**. She **believed** that plant life could **migrate** over time. She used maps to show where certain plants lived at different times. She showed that some plants had moved to different areas over many years.

Lucy Becomes a Teacher

In 1917, Lucy began to teach botany. She lived with her sister. They continued their scientific **behaviors**. Lucy took care of many plants. She **tended** indoor and outdoor gardens. Annette studied moths that fluttered in a **flurry** of wings around lights outside.

Lucy collected and photographed plants from around the country. Color photography was new at the time. She used the colorful photographs in her classes.

(bkgd) RoseAnn Hayes; (inset) J.S. Peterson/USDA

Lucy's Plants

Later in her life, Lucy wrote field guides. Field guides are books that help people tell plants apart. In 1950, she **published** an important guide. It describes forest plants in the eastern United States. Ecologists still use this helpful guide. It helps them study changes in forests.

Today, Lucy has a few plants named after her. One is called Lucy Braun's snakeroot. Scientists are worried this plant could become extinct, or disappear. Lucy's research on forest plants may help them prevent this plant's **disappearance**.

Lucy Braun lived to be 81 years old. She collected nearly 12,000 plants! Today her herbarium is part of the Smithsonian Institution in Washington, D.C. Visitors can study the plants she collected.

Plant Identification

Follow these steps to identify plants in your area.

Materials: a magnifying glass and a field guide

1. Identify the state or region and habitat where the plant grows.
2. Identify whether the leaf is evergreen or broadleaf.
3. Draw or photograph the leaf to record its shape.
4. Look at the leaves on the stem. See if they are opposite each other or not.
5. Narrow the list of possible plants in the field guide. Then find an exact match.

Text Evidence

1 Comprehension
Sequence

Reread the first paragraph. **Circle** the sentence that tells what Lucy did later in her life. What happened in 1950? Why is this event important to ecologists today?

_____

_____

_____

_____

2 Expand Vocabulary

When a book is printed and sold, it is **published**. **Draw a box** around the sentences that describe what Lucy *published*.

3 Purpose A C T

Reread the text in the box "Plant Identification." **Underline** the detail that tells what the steps will help you do.

111

Respond to Reading

Discuss Work with a partner. Use the discussion starters to answer the questions below about "Growing in Place." Write the page numbers to show where you found text evidence.

? Questions	Discussion Starters	Text Evidence
1 What did Lucy's mother teach Lucy to do to tell plants apart?	▶ When Lucy was a child, Lucy's mother taught her to… ▶ One way Lucy and her mother studied plants was to… ▶ I also read that Lucy learned to…	Page(s): _____
2 What did Lucy do when she was a teacher that helped her study plants?	▶ After Lucy became a teacher, one way she studied plants was to… ▶ To study plants from around the country, Lucy… ▶ I know this because I read…	Page(s): _____
3 What did Lucy do that helped other people tell plants apart?	▶ Later in life, Lucy helped people tell plants apart by… ▶ Lucy helped people study plants today because she…	Page(s): _____

Mike Moran

112

Write Review your notes about "Growing in Place." Then write your answer to the question below. Use text evidence to support your answer.

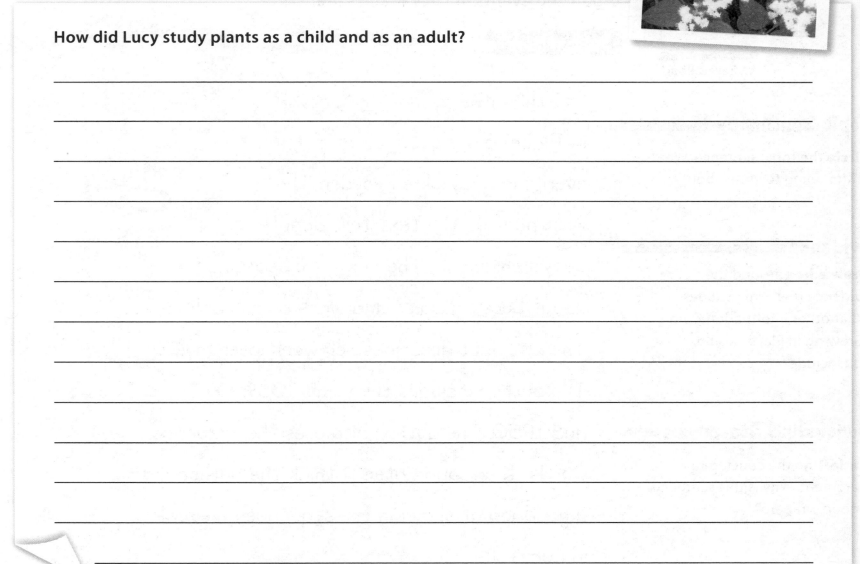

How did Lucy study plants as a child and as an adult?

_____

_____

_____

_____

_____

_____

_____

_____

_____

_____

Write About Reading

Shared Read

Read an Analysis > **Text Structure** Read Kim's paragraph below about "Growing in Place." She analyzes the sequence of events. She gives her opinion about how well the author organized events in Lucy Braun's life.

Topic Sentence

Circle the topic sentence. What is Kim going to write about?

Evidence

Draw a box around the evidence that Kim includes. What other information from "Growing in Place" would you include?

Concluding Statement

Underline the concluding statement. Why is this sentence a good wrap up?

Student Model

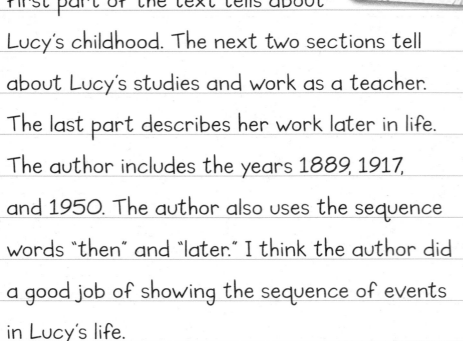

I think the author of "Growing in Place" did a good job of putting events in Lucy's life in order. The first part of the text tells about Lucy's childhood. The next two sections tell about Lucy's studies and work as a teacher. The last part describes her work later in life. The author includes the years 1889, 1917, and 1950. The author also uses the sequence words "then" and "later." I think the author did a good job of showing the sequence of events in Lucy's life.

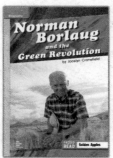

Leveled Reader

Write a paragraph about "Norman Borlaug and the Green Revolution." Review Chapter 1. Did the author do a good job of putting events in order? Tell your opinion and support it with evidence from the text.

_____

_____

_____

_____

_____

_____

_____

_____

_____

_____

Topic Sentence

☐ Include the title of the text you read.

☐ Tell your opinion. Tell whether you think the author did a good job of putting events in order.

Evidence

☐ Describe how the author organized events in the text.

☐ Give examples of time order words and dates.

Concluding Statement

☐ Restate your opinion. Tell whether the author did a good job of putting events in order.

Essential Question

When has a plan helped you accomplish a task?

Go Digital!

COLLABORATE

Write words to describe ways people can make a plan. Then tell why a plan is helpful.

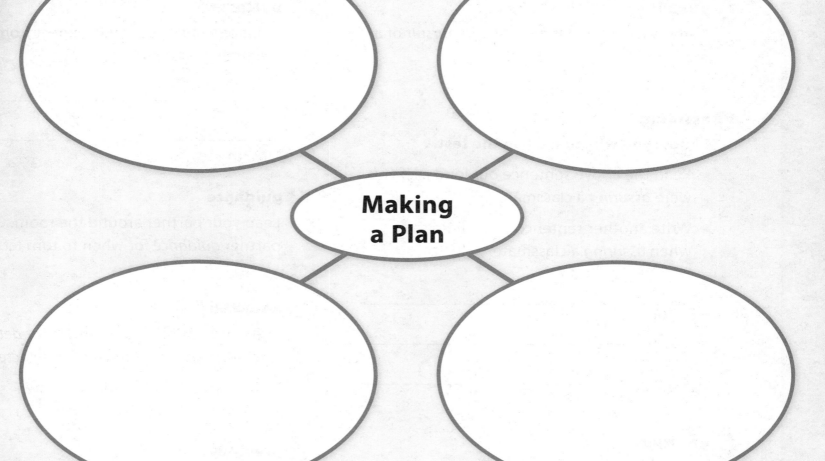

Making a Plan

Describe a time when you made a plan. What did the plan help you do? Use some words you wrote above.

Vocabulary

 Work with a partner to complete each activity.

1 pursuit

Name an animal that might be in *pursuit* of a mouse.

2 assuring

I know you will do well on the test.

▶ Read the above sentence out loud as if you were *assuring* a classmate.

▶ Write another sentence you would say when *assuring* a classmate.

_____

_____

_____

3 gratitude

Which of these are ways to show *gratitude*?

Give someone a small gift.

Read someone a story.

Thank someone for helping you.

4 outcome

What *outcome* would you expect from taking swimming lessons?

_____

_____

5 guidance

Lead your partner around the room. Give your partner *guidance* for when to turn left or right.

6 detected

The word *noticed* is a synonym for *detected*. Circle two other synonyms for *detected*.

missed   sensed   saw

7 previous

List two ways that you are different this year from the *previous* year.

_____

_____

8 emerging

Draw a picture of an animal *emerging* from its home.

High-Utility Words

▶ Homographs

Homographs are words that are spelled the same way but have different meanings.

Circle pairs of homographs in the passage.

I want to give my mom a (present) for her birthday. I want to (present) it to her at the party tonight. But Dad doesn't have time to take me to the store. So I will change an old can where I used to store my change. I will paint the can and Mom can use it as a vase. I will make her a great gift!

My Notes

Use this page to take notes during your first read of "The Magical Lost Brocade."

The Magical Lost Brocade

Essential Question

When has a plan helped you accomplish a task?

Read about how Ping follows a plan to find a lost brocade.

Long ago, in China, a poor woman and her son lived in a tiny hut. The mother wove brocade hangings and her son, Ping, sold them. She wanted to give him a better home, but that was **impossible** because she did not make much money. So she decided to weave a brocade of a magnificent home instead. It was her finest work. But soon after she finished, a wind swept into their hut. It carried the brocade away! The woman was heartbroken. So Ping went off in **pursuit** of the cloth, **assuring** his mother as he left and promising to return with the brocade.

Ping walked for three days and came to a house. A bearded man sat outside. "I'm searching for a brocade," Ping said.

"One flew by three days ago," said the man. "Now it's in a palace far away. I'll tell you how to get there and lend you my horse." Ping thanked him and bowed deeply to express his **gratitude**.

"First, you must cross through Fire Valley without saying a word," said the man. "If you make a sound, you'll burn! Then you'll arrive at Ice Ocean." He continued, "You must ride through the icy waters without shivering. If you shiver, the **outcome** will be terrible! The ocean will swallow you! When you come out of the water, you'll see the Mountain of the Sun. The palace sits on top of this steep peak. You will find the brocade there."

Text Evidence

❶ Expand Vocabulary

When something is **impossible** it cannot be done. **Underline** the text that tells what was *impossible* for the woman to do.

❷ Comprehension
Theme

Circle the details that tell what Ping does when the wind carries the brocade away. What does this detail tell about Ping?

_____

_____

_____

❸ Organization Ⓐ Ⓒ Ⓣ

Draw a box around the name of each place Ping will go on his trip. Will Ping's trip be easy or difficult? How do you know?

_____

_____

1 Expand Vocabulary

A **journey** is a long trip. How long was Ping's *journey* to Fire Valley?

_____

2 Comprehension

Theme

Reread the page. **Circle** the sentence that tells what Ping promises to do on his journey. **Underline** the sentences that show he met this promise.

3 Organization Ⓐ Ⓒ Ⓣ

Draw a box around the paragraph that tells what happens at the palace. What happens that was not a part of the bearded man's plan?

_____

_____

_____

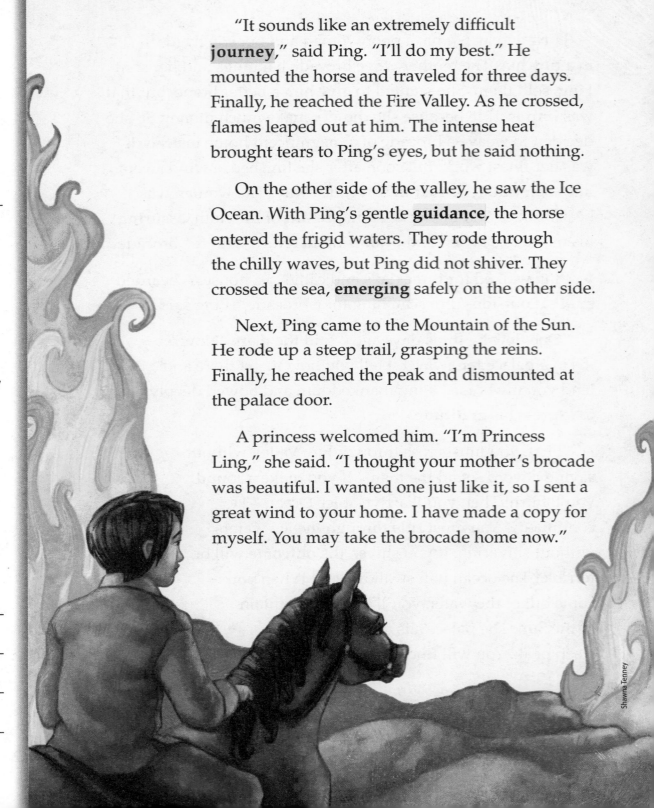

"It sounds like an extremely difficult **journey**," said Ping. "I'll do my best." He mounted the horse and traveled for three days. Finally, he reached the Fire Valley. As he crossed, flames leaped out at him. The intense heat brought tears to Ping's eyes, but he said nothing.

On the other side of the valley, he saw the Ice Ocean. With Ping's gentle **guidance**, the horse entered the frigid waters. They rode through the chilly waves, but Ping did not shiver. They crossed the sea, **emerging** safely on the other side.

Next, Ping came to the Mountain of the Sun. He rode up a steep trail, grasping the reins. Finally, he reached the peak and dismounted at the palace door.

A princess welcomed him. "I'm Princess Ling," she said. "I thought your mother's brocade was beautiful. I wanted one just like it, so I sent a great wind to your home. I have made a copy for myself. You may take the brocade home now."

Shawna Tenney

"Thank you," said Ping, who stared at the princess. She was very beautiful. He **detected** a knowing smile on her face as they said goodbye. He wondered if he could see her again.

Ping mounted his horse and placed the brocade under his jacket. First, he rode down the Mountain of the Sun. Next, he rode back across Ice Ocean, without shivering once. Then he rode across Fire Valley. He didn't make a sound. Finally, he arrived at the home of the bearded man, who sat outside just as he had the **previous** time. Ping thanked him, returned his horse, and began the long trip home.

Ping arrived home three days later. He had done his best and fulfilled his promise. "Here is your brocade, Mother!" he **announced**. Together they unrolled it, and the brocade came to life! Their hut became a magnificent house with gardens—and standing before them was Princess Ling! Ping and the princess got married. A year later, Ping's mother became a grandmother, and they all lived happily in their beautiful home and gardens!

Text Evidence

❶ Organization Ⓐ Ⓒ Ⓣ

Underline clues in the first paragraph that tell you that the princess and Ping will meet again.

❷ Expand Vocabulary

To **announce** means to state clearly and proudly. **Circle** the words Ping *announced*.

❸ Comprehension
Theme

What promise did Ping fulfill? **Draw a box** around the sentences that tell what happened to Ping after he fulfills his promise. What is the story's message?

_____

_____

_____

_____

_____

Respond to Reading

Discuss Work with a partner. Use the discussion starters to answer the questions below about "The Magical Lost Brocade." Write the page numbers where you found text evidence.

? Questions	**Discussion Starters**	**Text Evidence**
1 What was Ping's plan when he left home?	▶ When Ping left home, he planned to… ▶ I know this because I read that…	Page(s): _____
2 How did the bearded man's plan help Ping get the brocade?	▶ The bearded man helped Ping by… ▶ Another way the bearded man helped Ping was… ▶ The bearded man's plan was helpful to Ping because…	Page(s): _____
3 How did Ping accomplish getting the brocade and bringing it back home?	▶ Ping gets the brocade by… ▶ Ping brings back the brocade by… ▶ I know this because I read that…	Page(s): _____

Write Review your notes about "The Magical Lost Brocade." Then write your answer to the question below. Use text evidence to support your answer.

How did having a plan help Ping bring back the lost brocade?

_____

_____

_____

_____

_____

_____

_____

_____

_____

_____

Write About Reading

Shared Read

Read an Analysis **Theme** Read the paragraph below about "The Magical Lost Brocade." Connor analyzes repetition in the story. He tells how the author uses repetition to share a message, or theme.

Student Model

Topic Sentence

Circle the topic sentence. What is Connor going to write about?

Evidence

Draw a box around the evidence that Connor includes. What other details from "The Magical Lost Brocade" would you include?

Concluding Statement

Underline the concluding statement. Why is this sentence a good wrap up?

In "The Magical Lost Brocade" the author uses repetition to share the message that hard work leads to good things. Ping repeats actions to bring back the brocade. He has to cross Fire Valley without saying a word. He must cross Ice Ocean without shivering. He must do the same actions when he returns home. This shows that Ping works extra hard to get the brocade.

At the end Ping is happy. The repetition of Ping's actions shows that hard work leads to good things.

Leveled Reader

Write an Analysis **Theme** Write a paragraph about "The Lion's Whiskers." Review Chapter 3. Tell how the author uses repetition to share the story's message, or theme.

_____

_____

_____

_____

_____

_____

_____

_____

_____

_____

_____

_____

Topic Sentence

☐ Include the title of the text you read.

☐ Tell whether the author uses repetition.

☐ Include the story's main message.

Evidence

☐ Tell which words or events in the story are repeated.

☐ Explain how the repetition of details or events is a clue to the message, or theme.

Concluding Statement

☐ Restate how the author uses repetition to share the story's message.

Talk About It

Weekly Concept Making It Happen

Essential Question

What motivates you to accomplish a goal?

Go Digital!

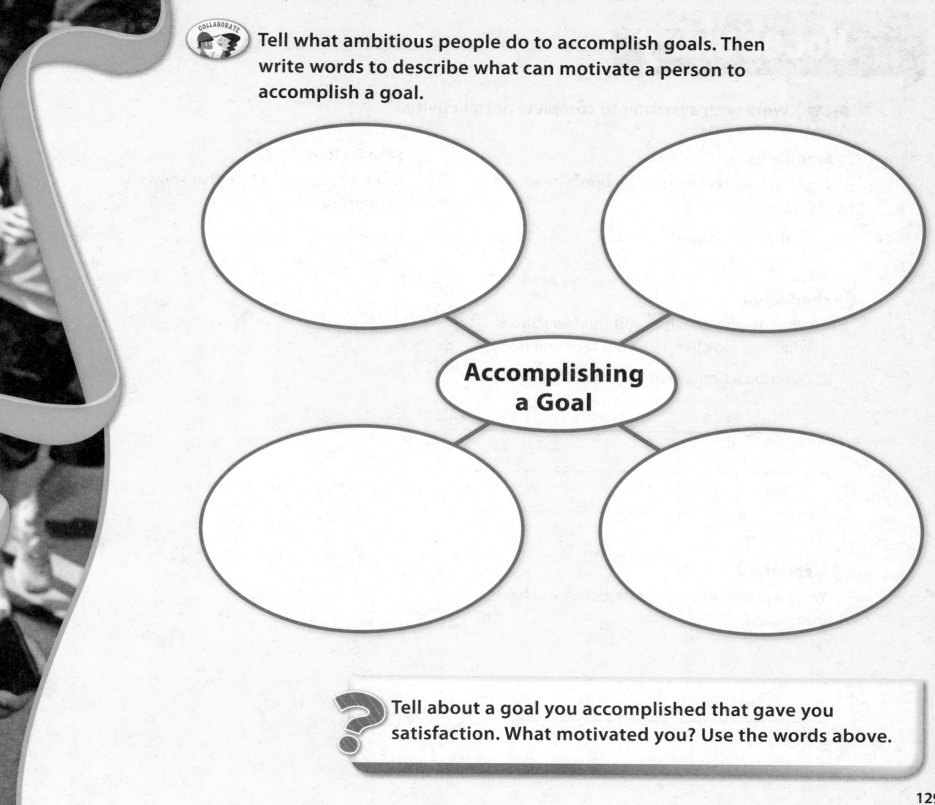

Tell what ambitious people do to accomplish goals. Then write words to describe what can motivate a person to accomplish a goal.

Accomplishing a Goal

Tell about a goal you accomplished that gave you satisfaction. What motivated you? Use the words above.

Vocabulary

Work with a partner to complete each activity.

1 ambitious

Circle a word that means the opposite of *ambitious*.

pushy   eager   lazy

2 shuddered

▶ What do you do when you *shudder*? Show what you look like. Use your face and body.

▶ Describe a time when you have *shuddered*.

_____

_____

_____

3 memorized

Write a phone number or date that you have *memorized*.

_____

_____

4 satisfaction

Draw a picture of a face that shows *satisfaction*.

130

Read the poem. Work with a partner to complete each activity.

UP TO BAT

Sara walked up to bat
and tugged down her cap.
Then she focused
on the pitcher, poised
with one arm raised.

Sara nervously held the bat
in her clasp.
Then she focused
on the ball
in the pitcher's grasp.

She pictured it flying high and then down,
like a bird diving for the outfield.
The pitcher threw the ball, and Sara swung—
struck—
and sprinted for a home run.

5 narrative

A *narrative* poem is a poem that tells a story. Tell the most important events of this *narrative* poem.

_____

_____

6 repetition

When a word or phrase is used more than once in a poem, it is called *repetition*. **Circle** a phrase that is used more than once.

7 rhyme

When two words *rhyme*, they end with the same vowel sound, such as *slip* and *trip*. **Underline** a pair of rhyming words.

8 free verse

A *free verse* poem does not have a pattern of beats or rhyming words. Is "Up to Bat" a free verse poem?

_____

My Notes

Use this page to take notes during your first read of "A Simple Plan" and "Rescue."

_____

_____

_____

_____

_____

_____

_____

_____

_____

_____

_____

_____

_____

A Simple Plan

Each morning when Jack rises,
He schemes a simple plot:
"I think I'll change the world," says he,
"A little, not a lot."
For neighbors he might mow a lawn
Before they know he's done it,
Or lead a soccer match at school,
And not care which team won it.
Some kids would laugh,
but Jack would smile
And look for more to do.
He'd walk your dog or tell a joke,
Or play a song for you.
Jack's brother John just didn't see
What Jack was all about.
John shuddered at Jack's crazy ways,
But Jack had not one doubt.

Essential Question

What motivates you to accomplish a goal?

Read how two poets describe unusual goals and why they matter.

"Who wants to do another's chores?"
John asked. "What does it mean,
'I'll change the world?' You're wasting time.
What changes have you seen?"
"Little brother," Jack explained,
"I used to think like you.
I thought, 'Why bother?' and 'Who cares?'
I see you do that, too.
I'd see some grass not mowed, or else
Kids not getting along,
And in the park no games to play—
I'd wonder what was wrong.
And then I had to ask myself,
What was I waiting for?
The change can start with me, you see,
That key is in my door.
I've memorized a thousand names,
And everyone knows me.
What do *you* do?" John had to think.
And he began to see.
Now each morning when Jack rises,
He hears his brother plan:
"I think I'll change the world," says John,
"If I can't, then who can?"

— Peter Collier

Text Evidence

1 Genre A C T
Poetry

Draw a box around dialogue in this narrative poem. Which character first says he'll change the world?

_____

2 Comprehension
Theme

Reread Jack's words. **Underline** key details. What lesson does Jack learn about making a change?

_____

_____

_____

3 Literary Elements
Rhyme

Reread the last four lines. List words that rhyme.

_____

Text Evidence

1 Literary Elements

Repetition

Reread the first two lines. **Circle** a word that is repeated.

2 Comprehension

Theme

Draw a box around details that describe the sea birds. Do these details show that the speaker feels hopeful or hopeless?

_____

3 Genre A C T

Poetry

A dash can show a pause in the speaker's thoughts. Reread the last three lines. **Underline** the line that includes a dash. What causes the speaker to pause?

_____

_____

_____

RESCUE

From the time we heard of the spill—
a *spill*, as if
someone tipped syrup
onto a tablecloth, as if
salt was shaken to the floor—
my coastal neighbors sailed out, flew
to find the sodden sea birds, bogged down
in waves of oil, a coating
so heavy no wing could lift.
From my own canoe I glimpse a head
once downy, but not drowned—
my heart holds hope!

BlueMoon Stock/Alamy

Reach, lift, and up—
it beats, this bird's heart!
I hold the sickened seagull, know:
Just as one spill can spell disaster,
One boat can bring back life.

— Elena Ruiz

Text Evidence

1 Comprehension
Theme

Circle details that tell about the speaker's actions. What do these actions tell about the speaker?

_____

_____

2 Genre Ⓐ Ⓒ Ⓣ
Poetry

Free verse poetry shares feelings. Look at the punctuation in the first two lines of this page. What feeling does the speaker express?

_____

_____

3 Comprehension
Theme

Draw a box around the speaker's message.

135

Respond to Reading

Discuss Work with a partner. Use the discussion starters to answer the questions about "A Simple Plan" and "Rescue." Write the page numbers where you found text evidence.

 **Questions**

 **Discussion Starters**

Text Evidence

	Questions	Discussion Starters	Text Evidence
1	In "A Simple Plan," what makes Jack want to change the world?	▶ Jack wants to change the world because he… ▶ He also wants to change the world because he… ▶ I know this because I read that…	Page(s): _____
2	In "A Simple Plan," what makes John want to change the world?	▶ John wants to change the world because he… ▶ I noticed that…	Page(s): _____
3	In "Rescue," what makes the speaker want to help after the oil spill?	▶ The speaker wants to help after the oil spill because… ▶ Another reason the speaker wants to help is because… ▶ I read that…	Page(s): _____

Write Review your notes about the poems "A Simple Plan" and "Rescue." Then write your answer to the question below. Use text evidence to support your answer.

What motivates the speakers in each poem to meet a goal?

_____

_____

_____

_____

_____

_____

_____

_____

_____

_____

Write About Reading

Shared Read

Student Model

Topic Sentence

Circle the topic sentence. What is Iman going to write about?

Evidence

Draw a box around the evidence that Iman includes. What other details from the poem would you include?

Concluding Statement

Underline the concluding statement. Why is this sentence a good wrap up?

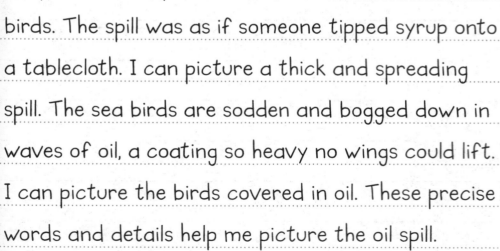

In the poem "Rescue," I think the poet did a good job of using precise language. The poet used words that helped me picture the spill and the birds. The spill was as if someone tipped syrup onto a tablecloth. I can picture a thick and spreading spill. The sea birds are sodden and bogged down in waves of oil, a coating so heavy no wings could lift. I can picture the birds covered in oil. These precise words and details help me picture the oil spill.

Leveled Reader

_____

_____

_____

_____

_____

_____

_____

_____

_____

_____

_____

Topic Sentence

☐ Include the title of the text you read.

☐ Tell whether the author did a good job of using precise language.

Evidence

☐ Include examples of precise language.

☐ Tell why the words helped you picture the characters or events.

☐ Include only details that create clear pictures in your mind.

Concluding Statement

☐ Restate your opinion about how the author uses precise language.

Unit 3
Getting from Here to There

The Big Idea

What kinds of experiences can lead to new discoveries?

Talk About It

Weekly Concept Cultural Exchange

Essential Question

What can learning about different cultures teach us?

Go Digital!

142

Write words that describe ways people can learn about the food, music, activities, and art of another culture.

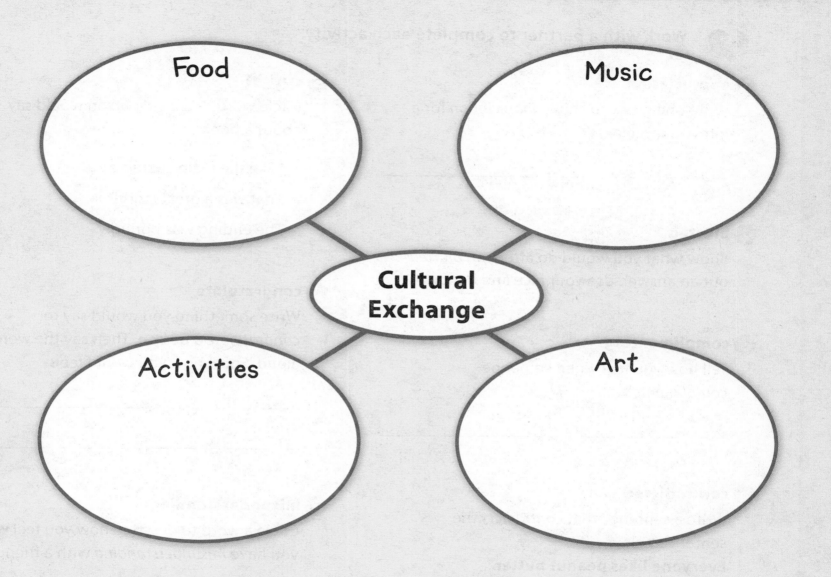

Food

Music

Cultural Exchange

Activities

Art

 Describe a time when you learned about another culture. Use words you wrote above.

Vocabulary

 Work with a partner to complete each activity.

1 appreciation

Write one way you show *appreciation* for a gift you receive.

_____

2 blurted

Show what you would do after you *blurted* out an answer. Use your face and hands.

3 complimenting

Tell how you feel when someone *compliments* you.

_____

4 contradicted

Write a sentence that *contradicts* the sentence below.
Everyone likes peanut butter.

_____

_____

5 critical

Circle words a *critical* person would say about a book.

I like the main character.

That was a great story!

The ending was boring.

6 congratulate

Write something you would say to *congratulate* a person. Then say the words aloud. Show how you would feel.

_____

_____

7 misunderstanding

Circle a word to describe how you feel when you have *misunderstanding* with a friend.

certain   happy   confused

8 cultural

Draw a picture of a *cultural* food or activity that you know about.

High-Utility Words

Contractions

A contraction is a short way of saying or writing two words. The word *isn't* is a contraction for *is not*.

Circle the contractions in the passage.

Jess and Marta are at a festival. "I (can't) see the floats!" Jess cried.

"We aren't close enough," Marta said. "I didn't think there would be a crowd!"

Jess sat on the curb. "I hope we haven't missed the band!"

"I don't think they have passed yet," Marta said. "Isn't it great that we'll see them up close?"

"Yes!" Jess said.

Sandra Baker/Alamy

145

My Notes

Use this page to take notes during your first read of "A Reluctant Traveler."

_____
_____
_____
_____
_____
_____
_____
_____
_____
_____
_____
_____
_____
_____
_____

A Reluctant TRAVELER

(bkgd) Panoramic Images/Getty Images; (l) Photodisc/Getty Images; (r) Westend61/Getty Images

Essential Question

What can learning about different cultures teach us?

Read about what Paul discovers in Argentina and what he learns about himself.

"I think packing winter clothes in August is weird," Paul said, looking out his bedroom window onto West 90th Street. This wasn't going to be a fun vacation. He was sure of it.

His mom **contradicted**, "It's not weird, honey. Argentina's in the Southern Hemisphere. We're in the Northern Hemisphere. So the seasons are opposite." To Paul, this was just another reason to stay in New York City. Paul wanted to spend the rest of his summer break hanging out with his friends, not visiting his aunt and uncle in a faraway country.

Paul's parents were teachers. They didn't have a **chance** to travel much. Now their apartment was covered with travel guides full of **cultural** information. They had been reading about Argentina since Aunt Lila and Uncle Art had relocated there. His parents had big plans. Paul, on the other hand, wanted to sleep late and play soccer with his friends. They lived in a city already, he thought. Why were they going to Buenos Aires?

As their plane took off, Paul's dad said, "Look down there!" Paul saw the island of Manhattan surrounded by water. Many hours later, as they were landing in Buenos Aires, Paul noticed the city was also by water and had bright lights, just like home.

Cartesia/Photodisc/Getty Images

New York City
Buenos Aires

Text Evidence

❶ Sentence Structure Ⓐ Ⓒ Ⓣ

Quotation marks " " mean that a character is speaking. **Draw a box** around words a character says in the second paragraph. Who is speaking? Who is the character speaking to?

_____

_____

❷ Expand Vocabulary

Having a **chance** to do something means having the possibility to do it. What do Paul's parents have the *chance* to do?

_____

_____

❸ Comprehension
Theme

Reread the page. What does Paul think about his family's vacation to Buenos Aires? **Circle** text evidence.

_____

_____

Text Evidence

❶ Sentence Structure

A colon : tells you that a list of things will follow. **Draw a box** around the list in the first paragraph. What is the first item in the list?

_____

❷ Comprehension

Theme

What does Paul think about the food at first? **Underline** what Paul's mom tells him. What does Paul do?

_____

_____

_____

❸ Expand Vocabulary

A **mood** is how a person feels. What does Paul say that is a clue to his *mood*? **Circle** these words.

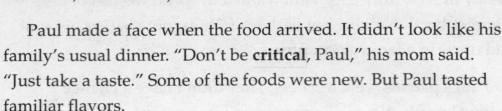

Aunt Lila and Uncle Art met them at the airport. They had a late dinner at a restaurant, as they often did back home. Uncle Art ordered in Spanish for everyone: *empanadas* (small meat pies), *parrillada* (grilled meat), *chimichurri* (spicy sauce), and *ensalada mixta* (lettuce, tomatoes, and onions).

Paul made a face when the food arrived. It didn't look like his family's usual dinner. "Don't be **critical**, Paul," his mom said. "Just take a taste." Some of the foods were new. But Paul tasted familiar flavors.

"I had something like this at César's house," Paul said after biting into an empanada. "This is really good." As he was **complimenting** the food, Paul felt his gloomy **mood** improving.

The next day was full of new sights, sounds, and languages. Paul noticed that like New York, Buenos Aires had people from all over the world. "We speak Spanish, but I really need to be multilingual!" Aunt Lila remarked.

On a plaza, Paul saw people dancing to music he'd never heard. Paul had seen break dancing on the street back home. He had never seen dancing like this. "That's the tango," Uncle Art said. "It's the dance Argentina is famous for! You're a soccer player, Paul. I know you have an **appreciation** for people who move well."

"That *is* pretty cool," Paul admitted.

Later, they drove to the most **unusual** neighborhood Paul had seen yet. The buildings were yellow and blue. "Soccer season has started," Aunt Lila explained.

"Huh?" Paul asked. He thought there was a **misunderstanding**. "Isn't it too cold for soccer?" he asked.

"It's nearly spring," his aunt replied. "Boca and River are playing at La Bombonera, the famous stadium, today. The two teams are rivals. Everyone watches them play against each other." She held out five tickets. Paul couldn't believe it.

"We're near the stadium," Uncle Art said. "People here have painted their houses in Boca colors."

"That's a great idea! Maybe I could paint my room in soccer team colors, too!" Paul **blurted**.

His mom smiled. "I **congratulate** you, Paul! Being open to new experiences is what this trip is all about. You've turned out to be a great traveler!" Paul smiled, too.

(t) Peter Horree/Alamy; (b) ©Marcos Brindicci/Reuters/Corbis

Text Evidence

❶ Sentence Structure Ⓐ Ⓒ Ⓣ

Circle a word in italics that shows emphasis. Read the sentence aloud.

❷ Expand Vocabulary

If something is **unusual**, it is different, or not like what you would expect. **Draw a box** around details that tell what is *unusual* about the neighborhood.

❸ Comprehension
Theme

Review Paul's thoughts about his vacation at the beginning. **Underline** details on this page that show what Paul thinks about Buenos Aires now. How does he change? What important lesson does Paul learn?

_____

_____

_____

_____

Respond to Reading

Discuss Work with a partner. Read the questions about "A Reluctant Traveler." Use the discussion starters to answer the questions. Write the page numbers where you found text evidence.

? Questions	Discussion Starters	Text Evidence
1 What did Paul learn about the food in Argentina?	► Paul learned that people in Argentina eat… ► When Paul tasted the food, he noticed… ► I know this because I read that…	Page(s): _____
2 What did Paul learn about the people who live in Buenos Aires?	► Paul learned that people in Buenos Aires come from… ► Paul learned that many people in Buenos Aires like to… ► Another activity Paul learned about is…	Page(s): _____
3 What did Paul learn about himself from his trip?	► During Paul's trip, I noticed that he liked… ► Paul learned that he is… ► I read that…	Page(s): _____

Buenos Aires

Write Review your notes about "A Reluctant Traveler."
Then write your answer to the questions below. Use text
evidence to support your answer.

What did Paul learn about the culture of Argentina? What did he learn about himself?

_____

_____

_____

_____

_____

_____

_____

_____

_____

_____

_____

Bernardo Galmarini/Alamy

151

Write About Reading

Shared Read

Read an Analysis ▸ Genre Read Emma's paragraph below about "A Reluctant Traveler." Emma writes her opinion about how the author creates realistic characters.

Student Model

Topic Sentence

Circle the topic sentence. What is Emma going to write about?

Evidence

Draw a box around the evidence that Emma includes. What other details from "A Reluctant Traveler" would you include?

Concluding Statement

Underline the concluding statement. Why is this sentence a good wrap-up?

In "A Reluctant Traveler," I think the author does a good job of creating realistic characters. Paul's parents are excited to go on vacation. Paul would rather stay home and play with his friends. Real kids don't always want to do what their parents want to do. In Buenos Aires, Paul's mom tells him to taste new foods. This is what a real parent might say. Paul finds things he thinks are cool, like street dancers. This is something that a real kid would like. I think these details show that Paul and his family are realistic characters.

Leveled Reader

Write an Analysis **Genre** Write a paragraph about a chapter from "All the Way from Europe." Tell your opinion about how the author creates realistic characters.

_____

_____

_____

_____

_____

_____

_____

_____

_____

_____

_____

_____

_____

Topic Sentence

☐ Include the title of the text you read.

☐ Tell whether you think the author did a good job of creating realistic characters.

Evidence

☐ Include three details about what characters do and say.

☐ Explain why each detail is realistic.

Concluding Statement

☐ Restate your opinion about how the author creates realistic characters.

153

Talk About It

Weekly Concept Being Resourceful

Essential Question

How can learning about nature be useful?

Go Digital!

Write words to describe how the person in the photograph is using nature.

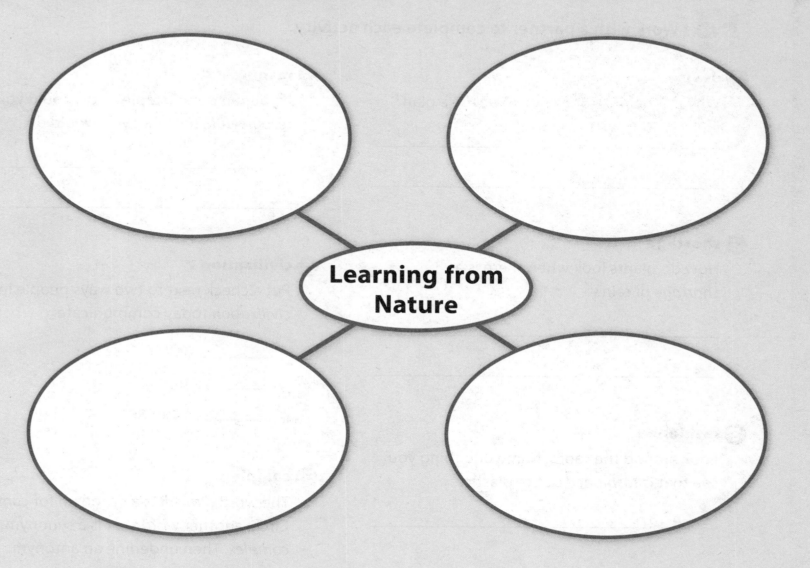

Learning from Nature

 Describe a time when you have used what you know about nature to help you. Use some of the words you wrote above.

Vocabulary

1 devise

Why is it helpful for a cook to *devise* a plan?

_____

_____

2 shortage

How do plants look when there is a *shortage* of rain?

_____

_____

3 fashioned

Look around the room. Name one thing you see that is *fashioned* out of plastic.

_____

4 tormentors

Circle two words below that describe what a *tormentor* would do.

   tease   annoy   hug

5 resourceful

If you ran out of staples, how could you be *resourceful*? Tell what you would do.

_____

_____

6 civilization

Put a check next to two ways people in a *civilization* today communicate.

_____ letter

_____ e-mail

_____ scribbles

7 complex

The word *difficult* is a synonym for *complex*. Circle another word that is a synonym for *complex*. Then underline an antonym.

   simple   puzzling   tiny

8 **cultivate**

Draw a picture of tree. Then draw a picture to show how a person would *cultivate* the tree.

High-Utility Words

▶ Homophones

Homophones are words that sound the same but have different meanings. Sometimes they have different spellings.

Circle the homophones in the passage.

Cal and Becca are outside (their) house. They hear a noise. "Look up (there)," Becca says. "From here, I can see a woodpecker."

"Oh no! It's making a hole with its beak!" Cal says. "What can we do so it won't hurt the whole tree?"

"I know that shiny things can scare woodpeckers away." Becca replies. "I'll buy some foil and hang it by the hole."

My Notes

Use this page to take notes during your first read of "Survivaland."

_____

_____

_____

_____

_____

_____

_____

_____

_____

_____

_____

_____

_____

_____

Survivaland

Essential Question

How can learning about nature be useful?

Read how four friends use their knowledge of nature to survive in a game.

"I'm going to win *Survivaland*!" Raul declared, starting the computer game. His character sprang into action on the screen. He raced across the desert island, chased by a sandstorm.

"Not today," Latrice said. "I'll come up with a way to be the last player standing!"

"No way," Juanita insisted. "I'll **devise** a winning plan."

Jackson frowned. "*Survivaland* is too **complex**," he complained. "It's too hard to have to know all about nature to win. In real life, knowing about nature is just not that important."

"You are *so* wrong!" Juanita cried.

They heard a loud *crackle*, and the entire room went dark. When the lights returned seconds later, the four players were very **confused**. Instead of controlling their characters on the computer screen, they were on the island themselves!

"We're inside the game!" Raul exclaimed. "And this sandstorm is blinding me! What should we do?" Suddenly, a sign in the sky flashed a message: RUN WEST.

"Which way is west?" Jackson called.

"I know," Latrice exclaimed, pointing. "The sun is rising over there, and since the sun rises in the east and sets in the west, west must be in the opposite direction."

Maryn Roos

Text Evidence

❶ Comprehension
Theme

Why does Jackson think *Survivaland* is too complex? **Circle** text evidence to support your answer.

_____

_____

_____

❷ Expand Vocabulary

If you are **confused**, you don't understand what is happening. **Draw a box** around details that tell why the four characters were *confused*.

❸ Genre Ⓐ Ⓒ Ⓣ
Fantasy

A fantasy includes details and events that are not possible in real life. Reread the seventh paragraph. **Underline** details that tell you that this story is a fantasy.

Text Evidence

❶ Expand Vocabulary

Something that is **gigantic** is very large. **Underline** a clue to the meaning of the word in the text. What other animal in the story is *gigantic*?

_____

❷ Comprehension
Theme

What does Raul know about butterflies? **Circle** three details. How does this information help the characters?

_____

_____

_____

❸ Genre A C T
Fantasy

Reread the last paragraph. **Draw a box** around an event that is not possible in real life.

The four players ran until the sandstorm was behind them. "Whew, that was close!" Raul gasped with a **shortage** of breath.

Suddenly Juanita shouted, "There's new trouble above!" The group looked up to see what the trouble was. They saw a **gigantic** butterfly. Juanita feared the monster-sized insect might fly down and land on her head.

Just then, Raul spotted onions growing nearby. He pulled an onion up and smashed it to break the thick outer layer. Then he **fashioned** the pieces of onion together into a cluster, and said, "Rub this all over yourselves. NOW!"

The butterfly floated down and touched Juanita with its feet, just as she had feared. She shrieked and the butterfly flew away. "I think my screaming scared it off," Juanita sighed.

"No, the onion did," Raul explained. "Butterflies like sweet flowers. In science class, we learned that butterflies taste with their feet, so I knew that the taste of a bitter onion would make the butterfly go away."

"I guess I was daydreaming that day." Jackson said. "Raul, I'm glad you're here to help us. You're a **resourceful** friend!"

Then a huge crow flew down and announced, "I'm hungry!" When the very large bird walked close to Jackson, Juanita tore off her silver bracelet and ring and threw them. The crow raced after the jewelry, and the friends ran the other way.

They kept running. Jackson called to Juanita, "Why did you throw away your jewelry?"

"I read in a nature book that crows are attracted to shiny objects. So I knew the giant bird would fly after the shiny jewelry!" Juanita explained.

"You see?" Raul said, looking at Jackson. "Knowing about nature saved us from our **tormentors** again."

The four friends kept on running, but only until they tripped over a log. They landed in gooey mud that covered their faces and made it impossible for them to see. They heard another loud crackle. When they wiped the mud away and opened their eyes, they were back in Raul's house! The mud was gone, and the electric blue sky had become the four white walls of Raul's game room.

"We're off the island!" Latrice cried. "We survived *Survivaland*! We've returned to a **normal civilization**!"

"So who won the game?" Raul wondered.

Jackson declared, "I think we all did—but I feel like the biggest winner because you've helped me **cultivate** a new appreciation for nature. And I want to keep learning more."

"Agreed!" the friends cried, as they wondered what game they might like to play next.

Maryn Roos

Text Evidence

1 Genre (A)(C)(T)
Fantasy

Draw a box around an event that could not happen in real life. Why is this event important?

_____

_____

2 Expand Vocabulary

Something that is **normal** is familiar or usual. **Underline** a clue that tells you the characters have returned to *normal* civilization.

3 Comprehension
Theme

Think about what Jackson says about nature at the beginning of the story. **Circle** what Jackson says about nature on this page. What lesson does Jackson learn?

_____

_____

161

Discuss Work with a partner. Read the questions about "Survivaland." Use the discussion starters to answer the questions. Write the page numbers where you found text evidence.

? Questions	**Discussion Starters**	**Text Evidence**
1 How does Latrice help her friends get away from the sandstorm?	▶ Latrice knows that the sun… ▶ Latrice knows which direction to run because … ▶ She helps her friends by…	Page(s): _____
2 How does Raul's knowledge about butterflies help his friends?	▶ Raul knows that butterflies… ▶ Raul helps his friends by… ▶ I read that the giant butterfly goes away because…	Page(s): _____
3 How does Juanita help her friends get away from the hungry crow?	▶ When the hungry crow walks close to Jackson, Juanita helps by… ▶ Juanita knows that … ▶ The friends get away from the crow because …	Page(s): _____

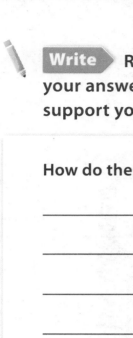

Write Review your notes about "Survivaland." Then write your answer to the question below. Use text evidence to support your answer.

How do the characters use what they know about nature to help each other?

_____

_____

_____

_____

_____

_____

_____

_____

_____

_____

_____

Write About Reading

Shared Read

Read Leo's paragraph below about "Survivaland." Leo writes his opinion about which event in the story is the most important.

Topic Sentence

Circle the topic sentence. What is Leo going to write about?

Evidence

Draw a box around the evidence that Leo includes. What other details from "Survivaland" would you include?

Concluding Statement

Underline the concluding statement. Why is this sentence a good wrap-up?

Student Model

I think the most important event is at the beginning of "Survivaland." After the lights go out, the friends are inside the computer game. The friends have to help each other to survive. They use what they know about nature. This makes Jackson see that knowing about nature can be helpful. The most important event is when the friends go inside the game because it causes Jackson to think about nature in a new way.

Leveled Reader

_____

_____

_____

_____

_____

_____

_____

_____

_____

_____

_____

Topic Sentence

☐ Include the title of the text you read.

☐ Tell your opinion about whether the most important event takes place at the beginning, middle, or end.

Evidence

☐ Describe the details of the event.

☐ Explain why you think it is the most important event in the story.

Concluding Statement

☐ Restate your opinion. Tell why the event you chose is the most important.

165

Talk About It

Essential Question

Where can you find patterns in nature?

Go Digital!

Write words that describe the patterns you see in the photograph.

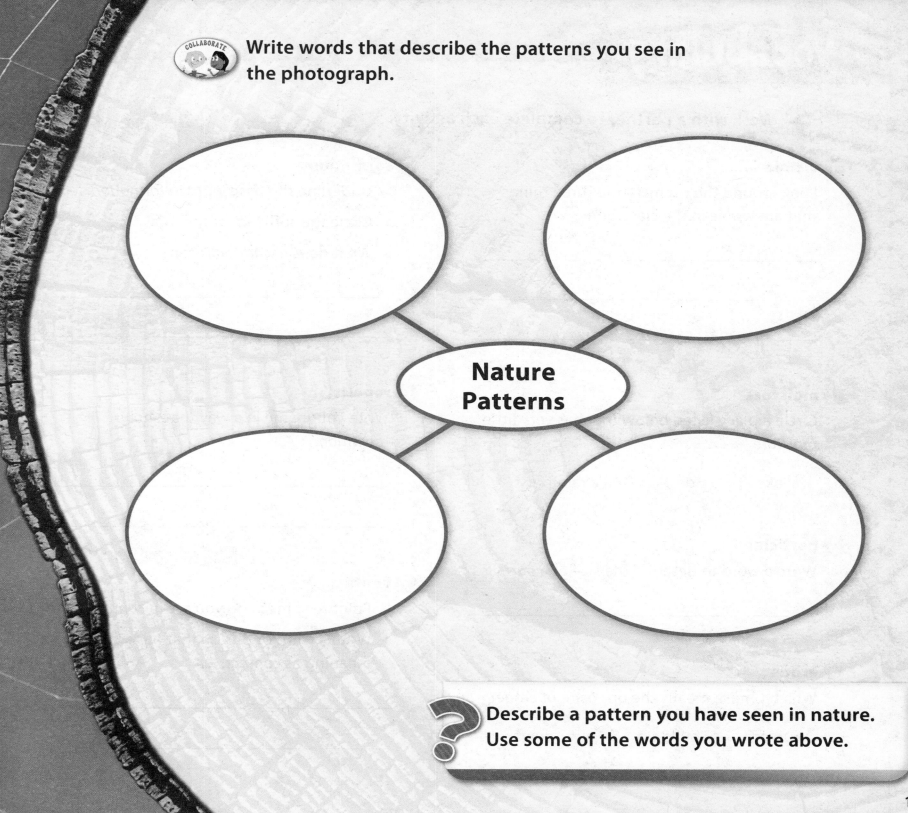

Nature Patterns

Describe a pattern you have seen in nature. Use some of the words you wrote above.

Vocabulary

 Work with a partner to complete each activity.

1 visible

Look around the room. Name three things that are *visible* in the classroom.

_____

_____

_____

2 moisture

Circle a place listed below that has very little *moisture*.

a lake   a desert   a rainforest

3 particles

Write a word to describe the size of a *particle*.

_____

4 erode

Which phrase means the opposite of *erode*?

rub off   build up   wear down

5 formation

▶ Underline the base word in *formation*.

▶ Circle the suffix *-ation*.

▶ What does *formation* mean?

_____

_____

6 repetition

Write your name in a way that shows *repetition*.

_____

_____

7 contact

▶ Point to something you are in *contact* with.

▶ Write a word or phrase that has a similar meaning as *contact*.

_____

_____

8 structure

Draw a picture of a *structure* you would see at a playground.

High-Utility Words

▶ **Prepositions**

Prepositions are words that show direction or location.

Circle the prepositions in the passage.

Jack and his dad went camping. They woke early and hiked (toward) a cave. When they were near the cave, they saw the cave was very dark. They went through the opening. Suddenly, they heard something fly over them. "Bats!" shouted Jack. They both rushed from the cave. When they got home, they told Jack's mom about their adventure.

My Notes

Use this page to take notes during your first read of "Patterns of Change."

_____

_____

_____

_____

_____

_____

_____

_____

_____

_____

_____

Patterns of Change

Essential Question

Where can you find patterns in nature?

Read about patterns you can find in rocks and rock formations.

Rocks Take Shape

"Solid as a rock" is a saying used to describe something that doesn't change. But, in fact, rocks do change. Water, wind, and temperature slowly turn one type of rock into another type of rock. These forces shape landscapes and sketch designs on rock. Patterns can form. Patterns are **visible** in rocks as small as pebbles and in the walls of the vast Grand Canyon.

The photograph across these pages shows one pattern that can be seen in a landscape. This **structure** of rock is known as the Wave **formation**. It was created by sand. The sand turned to rock over a long period of time.

Igneous Rocks

Igneous rocks are one type of rock. They are formed from hot, liquid rock called magma. Magma exists far below Earth's surface. Magma sometimes escapes to the surface through cracks, such as the mouths of volcanoes. When magma reaches the surface, it is called lava.

Lava is made of minerals. The minerals in the lava cool, and they form crystals. Eventually, the hot liquid hardens into a solid rock.

Igneous rocks can have different **textures** and colors. Granite is a kind of igneous rock that feels rough and can be many colors. Obsidian is another kind of igneous rock. This kind of rock is smooth and often black.

Granite

Obsidian

(bkgd) Stockbyte/Getty Images; (t) Sciencephotos/Alamy; (b) Natural History Museum, London/Alamy

Text Evidence

1 **Comprehension**
Main Idea and Key Details

Reread "Rocks Take Shape." **Underline** key details that support the idea that rocks change.

2 **Organization** A C T

What is the order of events that turns lava into solid rock? **Write "1"** next to the text that tells what happens first. **Write "2"** next to the text that tells what happens next. What happens last?

_____

_____

3 **Expand Vocabulary**

A **texture** is the way something feels when you touch it. Find words in the last paragraph that describe *textures*. List them.

_____

_____

Text Evidence

1 Expand Vocabulary

A **material** is something that can be seen and felt. It can be made up of one thing or many things. **Circle** the name of a *material* that is made up of bones and shells.

2 Comprehension
Main Idea and Key Details

Reread the third paragraph. **Underline** key details. What is the main idea of the paragraph?

_____

_____

3 Organization

How do sedimentary rocks become layers of strata? **Write "1"** next to the text that tells what happens first. **Write "2"** next to the text that tells what happens next. What happens after the layers build up?

_____

_____

Sedimentary Rocks

Limestone

Marble

Sandstone

Igneous rocks do not stay the same forever. Water and wind **erode** them, carrying away **particles** of broken rock. These tiny bits of rock may be carried to a beach, riverbank, or desert.

Over time, the particles collect. They form layers. The weight of the top layer pushes down on bottom layers. It squeezes out air or any drops of **moisture** in **contact** with the particles. Pressed together, the particles eventually stick to each other. They form a new **material** called sedimentary rock. This kind of rock can be made up of bits of rock, sand, bones, shells, and plants.

There are different kinds of sedimentary rock. Sandstone is formed from sand. Limestone is made up of bones and shells.

Rock Formations

Over time, a layer of one kind of sedimentary rock can form. Another layer of a different kind of rock can form on top of it.

Many layers of different kinds of sedimentary rock can build up. Each layer will press down on the ones below it. The oldest layer will be at the bottom. The youngest layer will be at the top. Layers of sedimentary rock are called *strata*.

Each layer can have its own texture and colors. These layers together can create patterns of thick lines in a rock. The lines can be straight or wavy. The patterns can be dazzling.

The Rock Cycle

As layers build up, the layers of rock below are pressed down. They are pushed deeper and deeper. They can go so deep that they are heated by magma. The weight of the layers and the heat cause metamorphic rock to form. Eventually, the heat will cause some metamorphic rock to melt. Then this rock becomes magma.

As the magma cools, it turns back into igneous rock. The **repetition** of this **process** is called the rock cycle. The rock cycle is a pattern. It repeats again and again. Liquid rock cools and becomes solid rock. Solid rock builds up from small particles into cliffs. Solid rock changes back to liquid rock, and the cycle starts over.

Rocks change by cooling, eroding, squeezing, and heating. Igneous rock, sedimentary rock, and metamorphic rock can all be broken into particles.

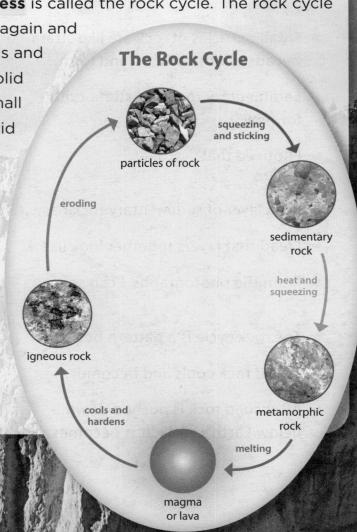

The Rock Cycle

particles of rock

squeezing and sticking

sedimentary rock

heat and squeezing

metamorphic rock

melting

magma or lava

cools and hardens

igneous rock

eroding

Text Evidence

1 Comprehension
Main Idea and Key Details

Reread the first paragraph. **Underline** three key details that describe how metamorphic rock is formed.

2 Comprehension
Main Idea and Key Details

Reread the second paragraph. **Draw a box** around key details. What is the main idea of this paragraph?

_____

_____

3 Expand Vocabulary

A **process** is a set of steps or changes that makes something else. What is one step in the *process* of the rock cycle?

_____

_____

173

Respond to Reading

Discuss Work with a partner. Use the discussion starters to answer the questions below about "Patterns of Change." Write the page numbers where you found text evidence.

 **Questions**

Discussion Starters

 **Text Evidence**

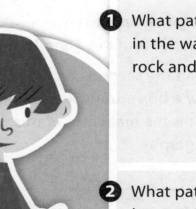

Questions	Discussion Starters	Text Evidence
1 What pattern is found in the way sedimentary rock and strata form?	▶ Small particles of rock are like strata because both build up and form… ▶ Sedimentary rock and strata both form by… ▶ I noticed that…	Page(s): _____
2 What pattern can be seen in layers of sedimentary rock?	▶ Each layer of sedimentary rock has… ▶ I read that layers together look like… ▶ From the photographs, I can see…	Page(s): _____
3 How is the rock cycle a pattern?	▶ The rock cycle is a pattern because… ▶ Liquid rock cools and becomes… ▶ After solid rock is pushed down below Earth's surface, it becomes…	Page(s): _____

Write Review your notes about "Patterns of Change." Then write your answer to the question below. Use text evidence to support your answer.

What patterns are found in sedimentary rocks?

_____

_____

_____

_____

_____

_____

_____

_____

_____

_____

Write About Reading

Shared Read

Student Model

Topic Sentence

Circle the topic sentence. What is Tisha going to write about?

Evidence

Draw a box around the evidence that Tisha includes. What other information from "Patterns of Change" would you include?

Concluding Statement

Underline the concluding statement. Why is this sentence a good wrap-up?

> The author of "Patterns of Change" used key details to explain how rocks change over time. Magma is liquid rock. When magma cools, it becomes solid rock. Water and wind carry away particles of rock. Particles collect. They form layers. The layers press the particles together. This becomes sedimentary rock. Layers of sedimentary rock build up. They push down the bottom layers. Eventually rock at the bottom melts and becomes magma. All of these key details helped me understand that rocks change over time.

176

Leveled Reader

Write an Analysis **Main Idea and Key Details** Write a paragraph about "Weather Patterns." Review Chapter 1. Tell how the author used key details to explain the main idea of the chapter.

_____

_____

_____

_____

_____

_____

_____

_____

_____

_____

_____

Topic Sentence

☐ Include the title of the text you read.

☐ Tell whether the author used key details.

☐ Tell the main idea that the details help explain.

Evidence

☐ Give examples of key details in the chapter.

☐ Include only the most important details that explain the main idea.

☐ Restate details correctly.

Concluding Statement

☐ Restate how the details helped you understand the author's main idea.

Talk About It

Weekly Concept Teamwork

Essential Question

What benefits come from people working as a group?

Go Digital!

COLLABORATE Tell how the group in the photograph is working together. Then write words to describe how working together helps them.

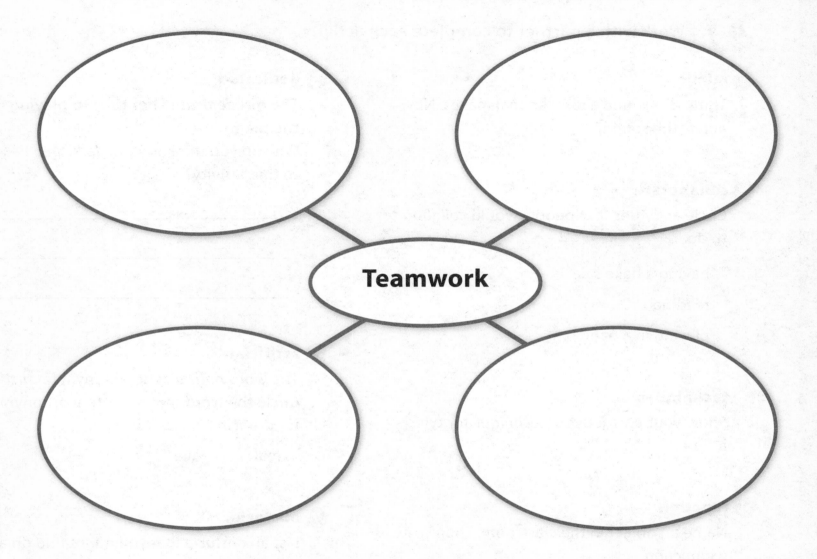

Teamwork

Describe a time when you worked with others. Tell how it helped you to work as a team. Use some words you wrote above.

Vocabulary

 Work with a partner to complete each activity.

1 mimic

Think of a sound a farm animal makes. Now *mimic* the sound.

2 collaborate

Circle activities that people would *collaborate* to do.

    having a bake sale

    reading

    playing in a band

3 techniques

Show your partner your *technique* for tying a shoe.

4 function

Name an object in the classroom. Then write its *function*.

_____

_____

5 dedicated

The girl *dedicated* her time to playing the piano.

Why do you think the girl *dedicated* her time to this activity?

_____

_____

_____

6 artificial

The word *natural* is an antonym for *artificial*. Circle the word that is another antonym for *artificial*.

    real   fake

7 obstacle

List an *obstacle* that you might find on a path through the woods.

_____

8 **flexible**

Think of an activity that you would have to be *flexible* to do. Draw a person doing this activity.

High-Utility Words

Possessives

A possessive shows ownership of something. An *s'* at the end of a word shows that two or more people or things own something.

Circle the possessives in the passage.

I went to a basketball game on Friday. The (teams') shirts were different colors. It was easy to tell them apart. Fans filled the bleachers. They waved flags. The flags' colors made the gym bright.

The gym was noisy. The coaches' voices were loud. The players' sneakers squeaked on the gym floor. The fans' cheers were also very loud. Everyone clapped for the teams' hard work.

B. Leighty/Photri Images/Alamy

My Notes

Use this page to take notes during your first read of "Gulf Spill Superheroes."

_____

_____

_____

_____

_____

_____

_____

_____

_____

_____

_____

_____

_____

_____

Gulf Spill Superheroes

Essential Question

What benefits come from people working as a group?

Read about how many people worked together after the Deepwater Horizon oil spill in the Gulf of Mexico.

Workers move material used to absorb spilled oil.

Fans of comic books know that it takes a team of superheroes to solve a problem. On April 20, 2010, a team of real-life heroes was called to action. An oil-drilling rig called the Deepwater Horizon exploded in the Gulf of Mexico. Massive fires raged above the waters. Down below, oil poured from a broken pipeline. Such a huge **disaster** would require the skills of many heroes working together.

The Deepwater Horizon oil rig was on fire. Fire boats came to the rescue.

Helpers in the Water

Right after the explosion, firefighters responded. They worked with the U.S. Coast Guard to put out the fire. Crews on boats and planes moved survivors off the rig before it sank.

Meanwhile, scientists tried to understand what was happening underwater. Each type of scientist had a specific job, or **function**. Some scientists studied water currents in the area. Biologists tried to protect animals from the spreading oil.

Most importantly, engineers came up with different ways to fix the broken pipeline. They discussed **techniques**. The leak was more than a mile below the water's surface. That was too deep for human divers to work well. **Experts** had to use robots. These devices had **artificial** arms and special tools to stop the spill. Many of the engineers' first efforts failed.

After nearly three months, workers fixed the damaged pipe. It would take many months to clean up the mess left behind.

Text Evidence

1 Expand Vocabulary

A **disaster** is an event that causes a lot of harm or damage. **Underline** clues to the meaning of *disaster* in the first paragraph. List two things that were damaged in the *disaster*.

_____

_____

2 Expand Vocabulary

People who are **experts** have great knowledge and experience in a certain subject. **Circle** the types of *experts* that helped during the Deepwater Horizon disaster.

3 Comprehension
Main Idea and Key Details

Reread the fourth paragraph. **Draw a box** around two key details that tell how experts worked to fix the broken pipeline.

1 Expand Vocabulary

When you **track** something, you watch it closely. What is a synonym for *tracked* in the first paragraph?

_____

2 Connection of Ideas

Draw a box around details that tell what veterinarians did. **Circle** what naturalists and ecologists did. How were these workers' actions similar? How were they different?

_____

_____

_____

3 Comprehension
Main Idea and Key Details

Underline key details in the last paragraph. What is the main idea?

_____

_____

Watchers from the Sky

From the water, it was hard to see where the oil was spreading. Workers had to **collaborate** with other groups, such as NASA space program. Satellites sent information to scientists on the ground. Weather experts **tracked** storms. They followed weather that might pose an **obstacle** to workers.

Crews in planes flew over the Gulf. Some crews told ships where to place barriers to protect areas from the spreading oil. Others brought supplies.

Heroes on Land

As the oil came closer to land, new helpers took action. Veterinarians **dedicated** their efforts to helping animals, such as pelicans and turtles. They spent time catching and treating animals that had been harmed by the spill. Then they returned them to the wild. Naturalists and ecologists cleaned up the animals' habitats. These groups often helped one another. Volunteers also helped out.

Workers catch a brown pelican. They will clean oil from its feathers and return it to the wild.

Local fishermen also needed help. They depended on seafood to make a living. Government workers checked fishing areas. They told fishermen where it was safe to fish. Bankers and insurance companies helped fishermen find ways to make up for lost income from seafood sales.

In Florida, experts worked together to come up with new ways to clean up the oil in the water. They needed to trap floating globs of oil that could ruin beaches. They created the SWORD, or Shallow-water Weathered Oil Recovery Device. The SWORD was a small type of boat. It had mesh bags that hung between its two sides. The boat could **mimic** a pool skimmer. It picked up oil as it moved. Because of its size and speed, the SWORD was **flexible** when cleaning up spills.

The oil rig accident required heroic efforts. In some cases, workers' jobs were very different. In others, their goals and tasks were similar. The success of such a huge **mission** depended on how well these heroes worked together. The lessons learned will be valuable if another disaster happens.

Workers set up materials to catch oil.

Text Evidence

❶ Comprehension

Main Idea and Key Details

What is the SWORD? **Underline** key details that tell how the SWORD works.

_____

_____

❷ Expand Vocabulary

A **mission** is a special task that a person or group of people decide to do. **Circle** words and phrases that help you understand the meaning of *mission*.

❸ Connection of Ideas

Reread the page. **Draw a box** around details in the first paragraph that support the idea that the workers are heroes. What did these workers save?

_____

_____

Respond to Reading

 Discuss Work with a partner. Use the discussion starters to answer the questions below about "Gulf Spill Superheroes." Write the page numbers where you found text evidence.

 **Questions**   **Discussion Starters**    **Text Evidence**

1 How did people work together right after the explosion?

▶ To put out the fire, firefighters worked with...

▶ Survivors were moved off the rig by...

▶ I know this because I read that...

Page(s): _____

2 How did people work together to help animals after the spill?

▶ After the spill, some people helped animals by...

▶ Other people helped animals by...

▶ I also read that...

Page(s): _____

3 What groups of people worked together to help fishermen?

▶ One group of people helped fishermen by...

▶ Fishermen were also helped by...

▶ I read that...

Page(s): _____

Write Review your notes about "Gulf Spill Superheroes." Then write your answer to the question below. Use text evidence to support your answer.

How did people work together to fix problems after the Deepwater Horizon accident?

_____

_____

_____

_____

_____

_____

_____

_____

_____

_____

_____

_____

Write About Reading

Shared Read

Read an Analysis ▶ **Main Idea and Key Details** **Read** Amar's paragraph below about "Gulf Spill Superheroes." Amar analyzed how the author uses key details to explain the text's main idea.

Student Model

Topic Sentence

Circle the topic sentence. What is Amar going to write about?

Evidence

Draw a box around the evidence that Amar includes. What other information from "Gulf Spill Superheroes" would you include?

Concluding Statement

Underline the concluding statement. Why is this sentence a good wrap-up?

The author of "Gulf Spill Superheroes" uses key details to explain how people worked together after an oil spill. Firefighters worked with the U.S. Coast Guard to fight the fire. Engineers discussed ways to fix the broken pipeline. Naturalists and veterinarians helped each other. They protected animals and their habitats. Experts also worked together to create the SWORD to scoop up oil in the water. All of these details helped me understand how different groups of people worked together after an oil spill.

Leveled Reader

Write an Analysis **Main Idea and Key Details** **Write a paragraph about "The Power of a Team." Review Chapter 1. Tell how the author uses key details to explain the main idea of the chapter.**

_____

_____

_____

_____

_____

_____

_____

_____

_____

_____

Topic Sentence

☐ Include the title of the text you read.

☐ Tell whether the author uses key details.

☐ Tell the main idea that the details explain.

Evidence

☐ Give examples of key details in the chapter.

☐ Include only the most important details that explain the main idea.

☐ Restate details correctly.

Concluding Statement

☐ Restate how the details helped you understand the author's main idea.

Weekly Concept Into the Past

Essential Question

How do we explain what happened in the past?

Go Digital!

Write words to describe ways people can learn about what happened in the past.

Explaining the Past

What event in history do you have questions about? Describe what you would do to find out what happened. Use some words above.

Vocabulary

 Work with a partner to complete each activity.

1 **preserved**

Which item has been *preserved*?

a photograph in an album

a letter in a garbage can

2 **archaeologist**

Which of these things is something an *archaeologist* would do?

dig to find remains of an ancient city

go to stores to look for new objects

put together pieces of an ancient pot

3 **historian**

Check two topics you would ask a *historian* about.

_____ outer space

_____ life in the American colonies

_____ the Civil War

_____ how mice find food

4 **era**

Name a president from an early *era* in American history.

_____

5 **remnants**

Name one *remnant* of a campfire.

_____

6 **reconstruct**

▶ Underline the base word in *reconstruct*.

▶ Circle the prefix.

▶ What does *reconstruct* mean?

_____

7 **fragments**

The word *parts* is a synonym for *fragments*. Circle two other synonyms for *fragments*.

bits   circles   pieces

8 **intact**

Draw a picture of a broken vase. Then draw a picture of the vase *intact*.

High-Utility Words

▶ **Indefinite Pronouns**

Some pronouns are indefinite, or do not tell the specific person, place, or thing they replace. *Many, some, a few,* and *all* are examples of indefinite pronouns.

Circle the indefinite pronouns in the passage.

Mr. Ryan's notebook was missing. (Many) thought it was still on his desk. Others thought he had left it on one of the tables in the lunchroom. All of us started searching, but no one could find it. Some checked the bookshelves. A few of us looked in the trash. Finally, Mr. Ryan found his notebook under a pile of papers.

kyoshino/E+/Getty Images

193

My Notes

Use this page to take notes during your first read of "What Was the Purpose of the Inca's Strange Strings?"

_____

_____

_____

_____

_____

_____

_____

_____

_____

_____

_____

? Essential Question

How do we explain what happened in the past?

Read two different views about the uses of a mysterious object.

Remains of the center of the Inca empire are found in Peru.

What Was the Purpose of the Inca's STRANGE STRINGS?

Strings of Numbers

The quipu was an ancient calculator.

Most of us use a calculator to do math problems. We also use paper and pencil. What if we didn't have these things? What if we had to add numbers with a tool that looks like a mop? Incas may have done this. The Incas were an ancient civilization in South America. The Incas invented the quipu (pronounced KWEE-poo). Most quipus were not **preserved**, so they fell apart. Only about 600 of these old objects are still **intact**.

A quipu is made up of strings tied to a thick cord. Two types of researchers—**archaeologist** and

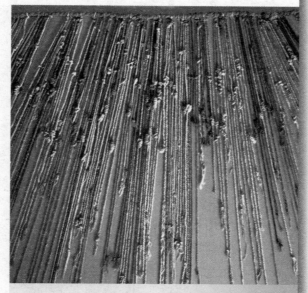

The quipu has puzzled archaeologists.

historian—have tried to figure out how the quipu was used. These experts believe knots on the strings **represent** numbers. Inca officials would count the number of crops in a village or the number of people in a house. They would tie knots on the strings to record the numbers. They could add up the numbers.

Text Evidence

1 Sentence Structure (A C T)

Reread the first paragraph. **Circle** the text in parentheses ( ). What does the text in parentheses tell you?

_____

_____

_____

_____

2 Expand Vocabulary

To **represent** means to stand for something. **Underline** the text that tells what experts think the quipu knots *represent*.

3 Comprehension
Author's Point of View

Reread the last paragraph. **Draw a box** around two details that support the author's position that the quipu was an ancient calculator.

195

Text Evidence

❶ Comprehension
Author's Point of View

Reread the first paragraph. **Draw a box** around details that support the author's position that the quipu was a calculator.

❷ Expand Vocabulary

The word **value** means the amount something is worth. Review the illustration. **Circle** the *value* of the first string.

❸ Sentence Structure Ⓐ Ⓒ Ⓣ

Text between a pair of dashes — — gives more detailed information about a word or phrase. **Underline** the sentence that contains dashes. What detailed information does it give?

_____

_____

_____

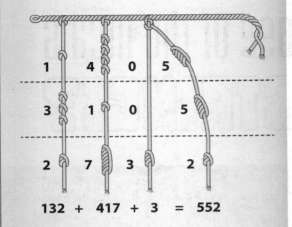

1	4	0	5
3	1	0	5
2	7	3	2

132 + 417 + 3 = 552

Top Knots = 100s
Middle Knots = 10s
Bottom Knots = 1s

Follow the illustration to understand how to count with a quipu.

A quipu would work like this: Clusters of knots would stand for ones, tens, hundreds, and thousands. The **value** of the knots depends on where they are on the string. If a cluster of knots is close to the top cord, it has a higher value. Incas could add up the knots to get the sum. They could also find the total of many strings or many quipus.

Patterns of knots on quipus are simply repeating numbers. If you add up the facts, it's clear the quipu was a calculator.

Strings of Words

The quipu was an Incan language.

The Incas were a mysterious civilization. In the peak **era** of the empire—the middle of the 1400s—the Incas built thousands of miles of roads, yet they didn't use wheels. They made houses of stone blocks but did not use mortar, a material that makes the blocks stick together. The biggest mystery may be how the Incas kept their empire together without a written language.

Researchers discuss a quipu.

The quipu may have been the solution. Only a few hundred of these **remnants** of the Inca civilization are still here today.

Quipus are made of strings that hang from a thick cord. On the strings are clusters of knots. Many researchers believe the clusters stand for numbers—though no proof from the past has been found. Others say that the knots are **symbols**, or a form of language.

Researchers found a three-knot pattern in the strings of seven different quipus. The order of the knots is the same on each quipu. They think the order of the knots is code for the name of an Incan city. They hope to use this and other patterns of knots to **reconstruct** the quipu code.

More proof that the quipu is a language comes from a text from the 17th century. Handwritten pages were found in a box holding **fragments** of a quipu.

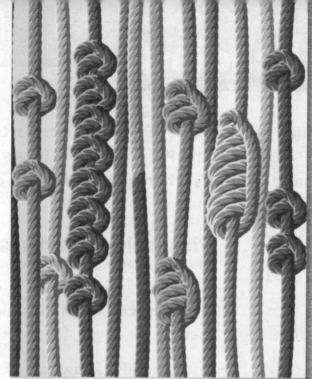

Some experts now believe that the quipu is not a calculator. They think the quipus' knots, colors, and patterns could stand for information about Inca history.

The writing says the quipus were woven symbols. The text even includes a list of words matched to some symbols.

The Inca empire spread over nearly 3,000 miles. Perhaps the quipu helped keep this vast empire together.

Text Evidence

1 Expand Vocabulary

A **symbol** is a sign or mark that stands for something else. **Circle** a word or phrase that is a clue to the meaning of *symbols*.

2 Comprehension
Author's Point of View

Draw a box around facts that support the author's position that quipus were used as a language.

3 Comprehension
Author's Point of View

Reread the page. **Underline** details in "Strings of Words" that are similar to details in "Strings of Numbers." How are the authors' views of quipus different?

_____

_____

_____

_____

Respond to Reading

 **Discuss** Work with a partner. Use the discussion starters to answer the questions about "What Was the Purpose of the Inca's Strange Strings?" Write the page numbers where you found text evidence.

❓ Questions	**Discussion Starters**	**🔍 Text Evidence**
❶ What do historians agree is true about the quipu?	▶ Historians know that the quipu was used by… ▶ Historians also know that the quipu is made up of… ▶ I read that…	Page(s): _____
❷ Why do some historians think the quipu was a calculator?	▶ Some historians think the quipu could be a calculator because… ▶ Another reason it could be a calculator is because…	Page(s): _____
❸ Why do some historians think the quipu is a language?	▶ Some historians think the quipu is a language because… ▶ Another reason it could be a language is because… ▶ I know this because I read that…	Page(s): _____

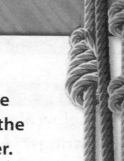

Write Review your notes about "What Was the Purpose of the Inca's Strange Strings?" Then write your answer to the question below. Use text evidence to support your answer.

How do historians think the quipu was used in the past?

_____

_____

_____

_____

_____

_____

_____

_____

_____

_____

_____

_____

Neil Stewart

Write About Reading

Shared Read

Student Model

Topic Sentence

Circle the topic sentence. What is Alexa going to write about?

Evidence

Draw a box around the evidence that Alexa includes. What other information from "Strings of Words" would you include?

Concluding Statement

Underline the concluding statement. Why is this sentence a good wrap up?

In "Strings of Words," I think the author did a good job of supporting the position that quipus are an Incan language. The author includes facts and details. Researchers found a pattern in seven quipus. They think this pattern is a code for an Incan city. A written text from the 17th century also says the quipus were woven symbols. The text matches woven symbols to words. I think all of these details support the author's position that quipus were used as a language.

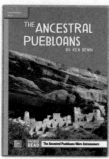

Leveled Reader

Write an Analysis **Point of View** Write a paragraph about "The Ancestral Puebloans." Tell your opinion about how the author supports his position that the Ancestral Puebloans were skilled builders.

_____

_____

_____

_____

_____

_____

_____

_____

_____

_____

_____

_____

_____

Topic Sentence

☐ Include the title of the text you read.

☐ Tell your opinion. Tell whether the author did a good job of supporting his position.

Evidence

☐ Give facts and details the author included.

☐ Include only facts that support the author's position.

Concluding Statement

☐ Restate your opinion about how the author supported his position.

IT'S UP TO YOU

THE BIG IDEA

How do we decide what's important?

Talk About It

Essential Question

What kinds of stories do we tell?
Why do we tell them?

Go Digital!

204

Write words to describe how the people in the photograph are sharing a story.

Sharing Stories

 Describe your favorite story. How do you know the story? Use some words you wrote above.

(l) redsnapper/Alamy; (r) Chris Vallo

Vocabulary

 Work with a partner to complete each activity.

1 deeds

Put a check mark next to each good *deed*.

_____ help someone carry a box

_____ tell a secret

_____ talk when someone is speaking

_____ lend someone a pencil

2 impress

Name a book or a movie that *impressed* you.
Why did it *impress* you?

_____

_____

_____

3 commenced

The word *begin* is a synonym for *commence*.
Write another synonym for *commence*.

_____

4 posed

Show how you would *pose* for a photograph.

5 exaggeration

Read each sentence. Underline the sentence
that is an *exaggeration*.

The tree next to my house is very large.

The tree branches are in outer space.

6 sauntered

Show how you *saunter* around the room.

7 wring

▶ Use your hands to show what you do to
wring out a towel.

▶ Why would you *wring* out a towel?

_____

_____

_____

8 heroic

Draw a picture of someone performing a *heroic* action.

High-Utility Words

▶ **Suffix** *–ly*

Words that end with *–ly* **describe an action.**

Circle the words that end with *–ly* **in the passage.**

Davy Crockett was strong. He also liked to help people, like that time when a storm (suddenly) came through town and knocked down the houses. Davy quickly built the town again. Then he bravely ran after the storm. The storm spun wildly. Davy calmly waited until the storm came close. He boldly threw a giant net around it and neatly wrapped it up. Everyone in town came out to thank him.

My Notes

Use this page to take notes during your first read of "How Mighty Kate Stopped the Train."

_____

_____

_____

_____

_____

_____

_____

_____

_____

_____

_____

How Mighty Kate Stopped the Train

Essential Question

What kinds of stories do we tell? Why do we tell them?

Read a tall tale about a young girl who saves the day.

Chances are y'all have seen a railroad train. Some of you may have even ridden one. But this story takes place back when railroads were still pretty new in the American South.

The star of this amazing tale is a young gal. Folks around here call her Mighty Kate. She got that name at birth because of how unbelievably strong she was. After the doctor weighed her on a scale, the tiny babe picked up the doc to see how much he weighed! **Deeds** like that showed just how mighty Kate was, and her nickname stuck like paper to glue.

Growing up, Mighty Kate continued to **impress** everyone with her great strength. If there was a boulder in her path when she was walking through the woods, she never stepped around it. She just tossed the enormous rock aside and **sauntered** along her way! Once, her pappy's horse and buggy got stuck in a ditch. Kate stepped in and pulled them both out—with just one hand!

But let's not get "off track" from the amazing railroad story you really should hear now.

One night, when Mighty Kate was just 15 years old, a **powerful** storm struck outside her home. Rain poured down, and gusts of wind blew so hard that houses shook in fear and trees ran for their lives! From her window, Mighty Kate saw a train carrying coal crossing Creek Bridge. Suddenly, there was a thunderous crash.

Jimmy Holder

Text Evidence

1 Comprehension
Point of View

Reread the second paragraph. **Circle** words and phrases that describe Mighty Kate. What does the narrator think of Mighty Kate?

_____

_____

_____

2 Expand Vocabulary

Something that is **powerful** has great strength or force. **Draw a box** around details in the last paragraph that show that the storm was *powerful*.

3 Genre ACT
Tall Tale

Reread the page. **Underline** three things Mighty Kate does that could not happen in real life.

Text Evidence

1 Genre Ⓐ Ⓒ Ⓣ

Tall Tale

Reread the first paragraph. **Draw a box** around three details that show that Mighty Kate is extra strong.

2 Expand Vocabulary

The word **ascended** means climbed. **Underline** words that help you understand the meaning of *ascended*. How did Kate *ascend* the vine to save the men?

_____

_____

3 Comprehension

Point of View

Circle words or phrases that show what the narrator thinks about Mighty Kate. What is the narrator's point of view?

_____

_____

_____

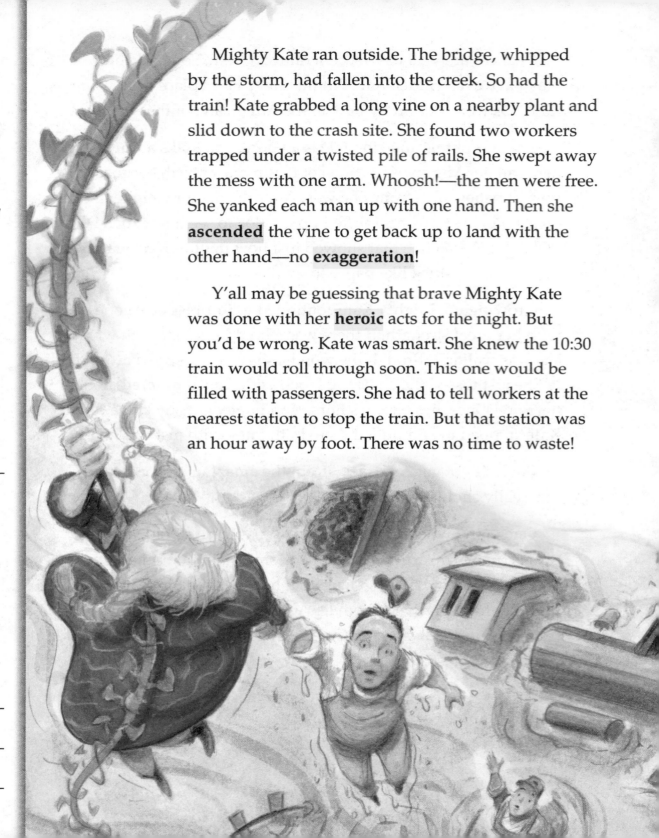

Mighty Kate ran outside. The bridge, whipped by the storm, had fallen into the creek. So had the train! Kate grabbed a long vine on a nearby plant and slid down to the crash site. She found two workers trapped under a twisted pile of rails. She swept away the mess with one arm. Whoosh!—the men were free. She yanked each man up with one hand. Then she **ascended** the vine to get back up to land with the other hand—no **exaggeration**!

Y'all may be guessing that brave Mighty Kate was done with her **heroic** acts for the night. But you'd be wrong. Kate was smart. She knew the 10:30 train would roll through soon. This one would be filled with passengers. She had to tell workers at the nearest station to stop the train. But that station was an hour away by foot. There was no time to waste!

With the wind and rain attacking her, Mighty Kate set out for the train station. Soon she came to River Bridge. It had stayed up through the storm. Kate **commenced** to cross the bridge. Floodwaters rushed beneath her feet. She wasn't far when, suddenly, she spotted a huge log. It was coming down the river toward the bridge—and Kate!

Mighty Kate leaned over the railing. She stood very still, as if **posed** for a photograph. As the log was about to strike, Kate grabbed it. She began to **wring** it with her bare hands. Pretty soon, that wet log was nothing but a twisted twig!

Mighty Kate ran across the bridge and on to the station. But the passenger train had already left. Kate raced after it but couldn't catch up. Then she got an idea. She whistled loudly—so loudly that the train driver heard it and stopped the train.

Kate ran up and told him that Creek Bridge was out. The driver thanked the brave girl who had saved the day. Because of her, the passengers were safe.

And because of Mighty Kate's good idea, today we have whistles on trains to give **warnings** along the track!

Text Evidence

❶ Genre A C T
Tall Tale

Reread the second paragraph. **Draw a box** around details that are exaggerated.

❷ Expand Vocabulary

A **warning** is a message or notice that danger is coming. **Underline** two sentences that tell the *warnings* Kate gives the train driver.

❸ Comprehension
Point of View

Reread the last three paragraphs. **Circle** words and details that show the narrator's point of view. What does the narrator think about the way Mighty Kate stopped the train?

_____

_____

_____

Respond to Reading

 Discuss Work with a partner. Use the discussion starters to answer the questions about "How Mighty Kate Stopped the Train." Write the page numbers to show where you found text evidence.

 **? Questions**

 **Discussion Starters**

Text Evidence

---

1 What events at the beginning of the story couldn't happen in real life?

▶ At the beginning of the story, one thing that couldn't happen in real life is…

▶ Another event that couldn't happen in real life is…

Page(s): _____

---

2 What does Kate do that makes her a hero?

▶ After the train crash, Mighty Kate helped by…

▶ Another way Mighty Kate helped people was when she…

▶ I know this because I read that…

Page(s): _____

---

3 What does Mighty Kate do during the storm that is amazing?

▶ One amazing thing that Mighty Kate did during the storm was…

▶ Another amazing thing that Mighty Kate did was…

Page(s): _____

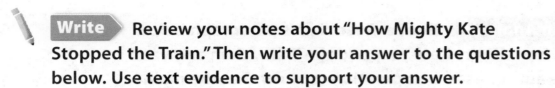

Write Review your notes about "How Mighty Kate Stopped the Train." Then write your answer to the questions below. Use text evidence to support your answer.

What makes "How Mighty Kate Stopped the Train" a tall tale? What is amazing about the story?

_____

_____

_____

_____

_____

_____

_____

_____

_____

_____

Write About Reading

Shared Read

Read an Analysis **Genre** Read Sam's paragraph below about "How Mighty Kate Stopped the Train." Sam analyzed how the author uses exaggeration to show that the main character is strong.

Student Model

Topic Sentence

Circle the topic sentence. What is Sam going to write about?

Evidence

Draw a box around the evidence that Sam includes. What other details from "How Mighty Kate Stopped the Train" would you include?

Concluding Statement

Underline the concluding statement. Why is this sentence a good wrap up?

In "How Mighty Kate Stopped the Train," the author uses exaggeration to show that Mighty Kate is strong. When she was a baby, she picked up a doctor. Mighty Kate also tossed an enormous rock. She pulled a horse and buggy out of a ditch with one hand. She swept away the mess from a crash with one arm. She pulled two men from a crash site with one hand. All of these exaggerated details show that Mighty Kate is very strong.

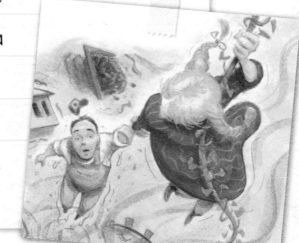

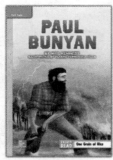

Leveled Reader

_____

_____

_____

_____

_____

_____

_____

_____

_____

_____

_____

Topic Sentence

☐ Include the title of the text you read.

☐ Tell whether the author uses exaggeration.

☐ Tell what exaggeration shows about the main character.

Evidence

☐ Give examples of exaggerated details.

☐ Include only exaggerated details that show the character's strength.

Concluding Statement

☐ Restate how the author uses exaggeration.

Talk About It

Essential Question

What can you discover when you give things a second look?

Go Digital!

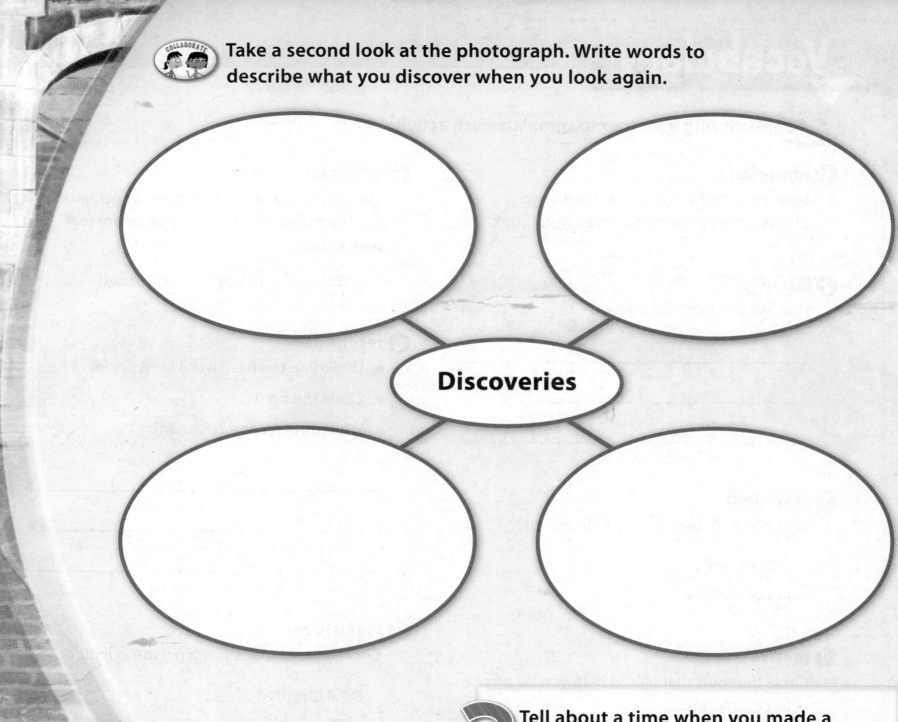

Take a second look at the photograph. Write words to describe what you discover when you look again.

Discoveries

Tell about a time when you made a discovery. Use some of the words above.

Vocabulary

 Work with a partner to complete each activity.

1 concealed

Look around the classroom. Name two places where you could *conceal* your book.

2 interpret

How do you *interpret* a yawn?

_____

_____

_____

3 suspicious

Which would make you feel *suspicious*?

people whispering

people talking

4 precise

Circle the tools that would help you be *precise* when measuring.

a bag   a ruler   a scale

5 perplexed

The word *puzzled* is a synonym for *perplexed*. Circle another word that is a synonym for *perplexed*.

certain   happy   confused

6 reconsider

▶ Underline the base word in *reconsider*.

▶ Circle the prefix.

▶ What does *reconsider* mean?

_____

_____

_____

7 inquisitive

Circle actions that show a person is *inquisitive*.

ask a question

tell a story

look up a word in the dictionary

8 astounded

Draw a picture of something you have seen that has *astounded* you.

High-Utility Words

▶ Words that Compare

Some words compare two or more things. Examples are *more, most, better,* and *best*.

Circle words that compare.

Mia and David's soccer team just won a game. "We played much (better) than last week," Mia said. "I think we had the best game ever!"

"Last week was the worst. We didn't play well, but the rain made it worse," David said. "We scored more goals today, too," he added.

"You scored the most goals!" Mia exclaimed.

Use this page to take notes during your first read of "Where's Brownie?"

_____

_____

_____

_____

_____

_____

_____

_____

_____

_____

_____

_____

Where's Brownie?

CAST

SAM *and* **ALEX JENSEN:** Twin sisters. SAM is outgoing. ALEX is quiet.

NARRATOR: One of the sisters, ten years later.

EVAN: A classmate.

NICK: The building manager.

NICKY: Nick's young son.

Essential Question

What can you discover when you give things a second look?

Read about kids who put together clues to find a missing pet.

Scene One

Setting: A bedroom in an apartment. SAM and EVAN are making posters. Nearby are a wet, torn paper bag and an empty glass container used to keep small animals.

Narrator: Whoever claimed that "two heads are better than one" never met my twin sister, Sam. Half the time, she makes problems worse rather than better. Like when we lost Brownie, our pet chameleon . . .

(ALEX enters. SAM and EVAN quickly cover up their work.)

Alex: How was the science fair? Did everyone like Brownie?

Sam: Mr. Rollins was **astounded** that my **exhibit** was so good. *(SAM tries to hide the empty container.)*

Alex: So where's Brownie? And why is Evan here?

(EVAN and SAM begin texting on hand-held devices.)

Alex: I'm not sure I understand what's going on. How do I **interpret** this silence? You're making me feel **suspicious**.

Sam: Um, Brownie's missing. But look! Evan and I made these. *(SAM pulls out a "missing pet" poster she had **concealed** with a book.)* We'll put them up at school. That's where I last saw Brownie. He was in that bag.

Alex: Hey, the bottom of the bag is all wet.

Sam: Maybe it got wet in the lobby. Little Nicky was playing in the fountain with the paper boats he makes.

Alex: That's *origami*, to be **precise**. Hey! The bag has a rip. Wait! That's it! I think I know where Brownie is! Follow me.

Elizabeth Buttler

1 Comprehension
Point of View

Circle the name of the Narrator's twin sister. What is the Narrator's name? **Draw a box** around details that describe the Narrator's view of her sister.

_____

2 Expand Vocabulary

An **exhibit** is an object or information shown for others to see. What did Sam show for her *exhibit*?

_____

3 Organization A C T

Reread the page. **Underline** the stage direction that tells what Sam and Evan do when Alex enters the room. Why did they do this?

_____

_____

221

Text Evidence

❶ Organization ⒶⒸⓉ

Circle details that describe the setting in Scene Two. How is the setting of Scene Two different from the setting of Scene One?

_____

_____

_____

❷ Expand Vocabulary

An animal that has **escaped** has gotten out of its cage or container. What did Brownie *escape* from?

_____

❸ Comprehension
Point of View

Where does Nick think that Brownie is? **Draw a box** around text that expresses his point of view.

_____

Scene Two

Setting: The lobby. A tall, green, potted plant stands next to a small fountain, where NICKY is playing. ALEX, SAM, and EVAN talk to NICK nearby.

Nick: I'm still **perplexed**. I don't understand why you think your lizard is down here.

Alex: Brownie's a chameleon. We think he **escaped** from the bag when Sam set it down near the fountain.

Nick: Hey, Nicky! Any brown lizards running around the lobby?

Nicky: Nope.

Nick: Maybe you should **reconsider**. Maybe Brownie isn't down here. Try searching your apartment.

Evan: *(checks his device)* It says here that chameleons climb trees.

Nick: Nicky! Any brown lizards in that tree?

Nicky: Nope.

Evan: It also says that chameleons love running water, like that fountain.

Nick: Nicky! Any brown lizards in the fountain?

Nicky: Nope.

Elizabeth Butler

Nick: I'm curious—what else does that thing say?

Sam: Yeah, **inquisitive** minds want to know.

Evan: Listen to this! Chameleons change color to match their environments when they're afraid or confused.

Alex: Of course! Nicky, any GREEN lizards over there?

Nicky: *(points into the tree)* There's just that one.

Alex: It's Brownie!

Sam: *(confused)* But Brownie has always been brown.

Alex: That's because we put only brown things in his cage, like wood chips.

Evan: Maybe you should buy him a green plant.

Sam: And a little fountain.

Nicky: And boats to go sailing!

Narrator: Well, that's how we found our **beloved** Brownie. Once we had our favorite pet back, everything was alright again!

❶ Organization Ⓐ Ⓒ Ⓣ

Underline the stage directions that describe Sam's feelings after Alex finds Brownie. Why does Sam feel this way?

_____

_____

_____

❷ Expand Vocabulary

When something is **beloved**, it is loved very much. **Circle** a clue to the meaning of the word.

❸ Comprehension
Point of View

Reread what the Narrator says at the end. **Draw a box** around words that describe Brownie. How does the Narrator feel about Brownie?

_____

_____

223

Respond to Reading

Discuss Work with a partner. Read the questions about "Where's Brownie?" Use the discussion starters to answer the questions. Write the page numbers to show where you found text evidence.

 **Questions**   **Discussion Starters**    **Text Evidence**

❶ What clues lead Alex, Sam, and Evan to look for Brownie in the lobby?

▶ Alex, Sam, and Evan go to the lobby because…

▶ I read that Alex notices…

▶ Another thing Alex notices is that…

Page(s): _____

❷ What clues does Evan find each time he checks his device?

▶ When Evan first checks his device, he finds out that…

▶ The second thing Evan finds out is…

▶ The last thing Evan finds out is…

Page(s): _____

❸ Why does Alex tell Nicky to look in the tree again?

▶ Alex tells Nicky to look in the tree again because…

▶ I know this because I read that…

Page(s): _____

Mike Moran

Write Review your notes about "Where's Brownie?" Then write your answer to the question below. Use text evidence to support your answer.

What clues do the characters discover that help them find Brownie?

_____

_____

_____

_____

_____

_____

_____

_____

_____

_____

Elizabeth Buttler

Write About Reading

Shared Read

Read an Analysis **Genre** Read Ava's paragraph below about "Where's Brownie?" Ava compared two characters and told her opinion about which character was a better problem solver.

Student Model

In "Where's Brownie," I think Alex is a better problem solver than Sam. Alex sees that the bag is wet and has a rip. She uses these clues to figure out that Brownie is in the lobby. Alex also uses information from Evan to help her find Brownie. Sam is not as good at solving problems. Sam was going to put up posters to find Brownie. She didn't look for clues to find him. For all these reasons, I think Alex is a better problem solver than Sam.

Topic Sentence

Circle the topic sentence. What is Ava going to write about?

Evidence

Draw a box around the evidence that Ava includes. What other details from "Where's Brownie?" would you include?

Concluding Statement

Underline the concluding statement. Why is this sentence a good wrap up?

Leveled Reader

Write an Analysis > **Genre** Write a paragraph about "The Mysterious Teacher." Compare two characters. Then tell your opinion about which character is a better problem solver.

_____

_____

_____

_____

_____

_____

_____

_____

_____

_____

_____

_____

Topic Sentence

☐ Include the title of the text.

☐ Tell which character you thought was a better problem solver than another.

☐ Be sure to include both character names.

Evidence

☐ Tell why one character is a better problem solver than another.

☐ Support your opinion with examples of the character's words and actions.

☐ Restate details correctly.

Concluding Statement

☐ Restate your opinion about which character was a better problem solver.

Talk About It

Essential Question

What can people do to bring about a positive change?

Go Digital!

UAW SAYS: END SEGREGATED RULES IN PUBLIC SCHOOLS

DECENT HOUSING NOW!

FEPC LAW NOW!

WE MARCH FOR FIRST CLASS CITIZENSHIP NOW!

Write words to describe actions people can take to make a positive change.

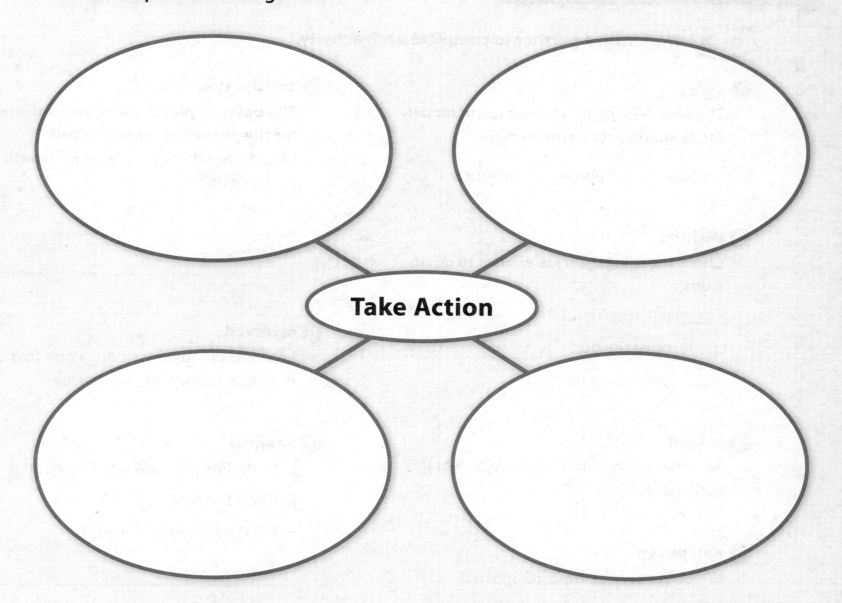

Take Action

 Tell about a person you know who worked to make a positive change. Use some words you wrote above.

Vocabulary

 Work with a partner to complete each activity.

1 defy

The phrase *go against* is a synonym for *defy*.
Circle another synonym for *defy*.

discuss   agree   disobey

2 entitled

Check the things you are *entitled* to do on
a bus.

_____ talk to a friend

_____ drive the bus

_____ get off at a bus stop

3 sought

Tell what information you have *sought* in a
dictionary.

4 outspoken

Which speaker below is *outspoken*?

Gina says, "We must raise money for the
animal hospital!"
Nick says, "An animal hospital takes care of
cats and dogs."

5 anticipation

**The baseball player waits with *anticipation*
for the pitcher to throw the ball.**
Why do you think the player waits with
anticipation?

_____

_____

6 reserved

Look around the classroom. Point to a chair or
desk that is *reserved* for a teacher.

7 unequal

▶ Underline the base word in *unequal*.

▶ Circle the prefix.

▶ What does *unequal* mean?

_____

_____

_____

8 **neutral**

Draw a picture of a person who must be *neutral* during a sports game.

High-Utility Words

Linking Words

Linking words join two ideas. Some examples are *if, because, so, when,* and *since.*

Circle the linking words in the passage.

My family offered to help Mrs. Lee (because) her dog went missing. Mom called all of the neighbors so they would look out for a dog. Dad and I put up posters since our neighborhood is big. When we got home, we heard that Mrs. Lee's dog had returned. A neighbor had found her. Mrs. Lee thanked us. "Duke might still be missing if you hadn't helped!" she said.

My Notes

Use this page to take notes during your first read of "Frederick Douglass."

_____

_____

_____

_____

_____

_____

_____

_____

_____

_____

_____

_____

FREDERICK DOUGLASS

Freedom's Voice

Essential Question

What can people do to bring about a positive change?

Read about what Frederick Douglass did to bring about positive change for African Americans.

Growing Up with Slavery

When Frederick Douglass was growing up in Maryland, he never could have imagined he would become a great leader. He was born Frederick Bailey and lived in slavery until the age of twenty. Frederick never knew his father and was separated from his mother at a young age. If he **dared** to **defy**, or disobey, his "master," he was punished. However, the wife of a slave holder helped him. She taught him to read. Perhaps it was his love of words, along with his courage, that inspired Frederick to try for the kind of life he was **entitled** to have. He thought it was his right.

New Beginnings

In 1838 Frederick **sought** his freedom by escaping to the North. In New York City, he married, and then he and his wife moved to Massachusetts.

Frederick changed his last name to Douglass to protect himself against slave catchers. He also discovered a group of people who shared his hope of ending slavery. They were called abolitionists. He had read about their movement in William Lloyd Garrison's newspaper, *The Liberator*. Frederick read every issue because the ideas inspired him. Soon he began speaking against slavery at church meetings.

▼ **This illustration shows a slave auction, a common event in the early 1800s.**

© Bettmann/Corbis

Text Evidence

1 Expand Vocabulary

A person who **dared** to do something had courage to take a risk. **Circle** the detail that tells what Frederick *dared* to do.

2 Comprehension
Author's Point of View

Reread the first paragraph. **Draw a box** around words and phrases that describe Frederick Douglass. What does the author think about Frederick Douglass?

_____

_____

3 Sentence Structure Ⓐ Ⓒ Ⓣ

Underline the title of a newspaper in the section "New Beginnings." What did Frederick Douglass read about in this newspaper?

_____

_____

Text Evidence

❶ Expand Vocabulary

A **gathering** is a group of people that come together for a reason. **Draw a box** around a synonym for *gathering*. What was the reason for the *gathering*?

_____

_____

❷ Sentence Structure

What feeling does the author express when Frederick begins his speech? What feeling does the author express after?

_____

_____

❸ Comprehension
Author's Point of View

Reread the last paragraph. **Circle** details that show what the author thinks of Frederick as a speaker.

An Important Speech

In 1841, the Massachusetts Anti-Slavery Society held a meeting. Frederick was eager to hear the abolitionist speakers. He went to the meeting with **anticipation**. When he arrived, an abolitionist who had heard Frederick speak at a church meeting asked him to speak to this large **gathering**!

At first, Frederick spoke quietly and hesitantly. He felt nervous standing in front of so many people—especially white people! However, once he started speaking, his fear went away. Frederick spoke clearly and from his heart. He was **outspoken**, describing the horrors of slavery. At the end of his speech, the audience immediately stood up and cheered! Among those cheering was William Lloyd Garrison.

After the meeting, Garrison offered Frederick a job as a speaker for the Society.

Frederick agreed to take the job. He felt he had found a purpose for his life.

Frederick traveled through New England and the Midwest, giving speeches that captivated audiences. It was impossible to listen to his powerful words and remain **neutral**. Frederick had a strong presence and expressed his opinions clearly and with dignity. He got others to support his ideas to end slavery. He was making a name for himself.

North Wind Picture Archives/Alamy

Making a Difference

Frederick also **reserved**, or set aside, time to write. In 1845, he wrote an autobiography, *Narrative of the Life of Frederick Douglass, an American Slave.* The book was a success and made him even more famous.

In his autobiography, Frederick revealed that he had run away from slavery. That was against the law. Slave catchers would be searching for him. For his safety, friends suggested that he go on a speaking tour in Great Britain. Frederick was very popular. People lined up to hear him.

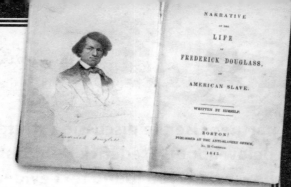

▲ Frederick's autobiography helped spread the idea of ending slavery.

In 1847, Frederick returned to the United States. He started his own abolitionist newspaper, *The North Star.* It published articles that were against slavery and the **unequal status** of women. Frederick thought women should be treated as equals to men in society. He also thought African Americans should not be separated from others in schools. He continued to work for these important causes throughout his life.

◀ *The North Star* was a newspaper. Frederick Douglass and his wife published it.

(t) Aurora Photos/Alamy; (b) Everett Collection/Alamy

Text Evidence

① **Sentence Structure** Ⓐ Ⓒ Ⓣ

Underline the titles of books or newspapers Frederick published. What kind of book did he write?

_____

② **Expand Vocabulary**

A person's **status** is their position compared to others. What was the *status* of women compared to men in Frederick's time?

_____

_____

③ **Comprehension**
Author's Point of View

Circle text that tells Frederick's views of women and African Americans. Does the author agree or disagree with Frederick? **Draw a box** around text evidence that supports your answer.

_____

Respond to Reading

 Discuss ▸ Work with a partner. Use the discussion starters to answer the questions below about "Frederick Douglass." Write page numbers to show where you found text evidence.

 ❓ **Questions**	💬 **Discussion Starters**	🔍 **Text Evidence**
1 What did Frederick do in 1841 to show he was against slavery?	▸ In 1841, Frederick went to… ▸ He showed his opinion by… ▸ I read that…	Page(s): _____
2 What did Frederick do to get others to support his ideas about slavery?	▸ One way Frederick got people to support his ideas was by… ▸ Another way Frederick got people to listen to his ideas was by… ▸ I noticed that…	Page(s): _____
3 What did Frederick publish about slavery?	▸ In 1845, Frederick wrote about… ▸ In *The North Star*, Frederick published… ▸ I read that…	Page(s): _____

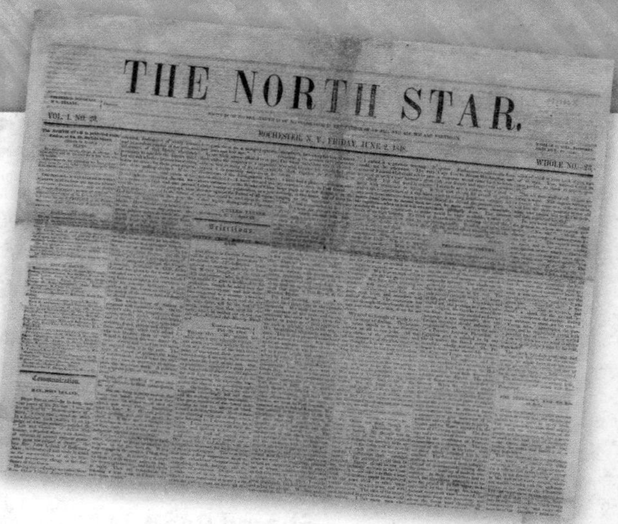

Write Review your notes about "Frederick Douglass." Then write your answer to the question below. Use text evidence to support your answer.

What did Frederick Douglass do to try to change people's ideas about slavery?

Everett Collection/Alamy

Write About Reading

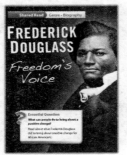

Shared Read

Read an Analysis **Author's Point of View** Read Eli's paragraph below about "Frederick Douglass." He analyzed how details in the text show the author's point of view.

Student Model

Many details in "Frederick Douglass" show that the author thinks he was a great leader. The author describes Frederick as outspoken. He used powerful words to speak out against slavery. People listened to him. He got people to support his ideas to end slavery. He started his own newspaper. He published articles against slavery and the unequal status of women. The author describes these causes as important. All of these details show that the author thinks Frederick Douglass was a great leader.

Topic Sentence

Circle the topic sentence. What is Eli going to write about?

Evidence

Draw a box around the evidence that Eli includes. What other information from "Frederick Douglass" would you include?

Concluding Statement

Underline the concluding statement. Why is this sentence a good wrap up?

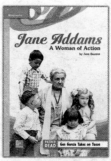

Leveled Reader

Write an Analysis   **Author's Point of View**   Write a paragraph about "Jane Addams: A Woman of Action." Review Chapter 3. Tell how details show the author's point of view.

_____
_____
_____
_____
_____
_____
_____
_____
_____
_____
_____

Topic Sentence

☐ Include the title of the text you read.

☐ Tell whether details show the author's point of view.

☐ Include the author's point of view.

Evidence

☐ Give examples of words and details that show the author's point of view.

☐ Restate details from the text correctly.

Concluding Statement

☐ Restate whether details in the text show the author's point of view.

Talk About It

Weekly Concept Consider Our Resources

Essential Question

Why are natural resources valuable?

Go Digital!

Write examples of natural resources you see in the photograph. Tell why each natural resource is important.

Natural Resources

 Name a natural resource that is important to you. Tell why it is important. Use some words you wrote above.

Vocabulary

 Work with a partner to complete each activity.

1 absorb

List two things that will *absorb* water.

_____

_____

2 affect

How does putting on a sweater *affect* your body?

_____

_____

3 circulates

Stand next to your partner. Then show how you *circulate* around each other.

4 cycle

Name something that happens in a *cycle* every year.

_____

5 glaciers

Circle words below that are related to *glaciers*. Then write another word related to *glaciers*.

    ice   grass   frozen   heat

_____

6 conserve

Which action below is a way to *conserve* water?

    turning on a sprinkler

    turning off a dripping hose

7 seeps

Read the synonyms for *seeps* below. Add one more synonym.

seeps: flows, trickles, _____

_____

8 necessity

Draw a picture of a plant. Then draw something that is a *necessity* for it to grow.

High-Utility Words

▶ Compare and Contrast Words

Compare and contrast words signal that an author is showing that two people, things, or ideas are alike or different.

Circle compare and contrast words.

Cars need energy to run. In the past, most cars used gasoline to run. Today, (however,) cars can get energy in other ways. Although, many still use gasoline, some cars use fuel made from corn. In addition, there are cars that can use electricity. Some use only electricity. Some use electricity as well as gasoline. Compared with cars long ago, cars today have many ways to make them go.

Werner H. Muelle/Corbis Bridge/Alamy

My Notes

Use this page to take notes during your first read of "Power from Nature."

Power from NATURE

Wind turbines are placed in open areas.

Essential Question

Why are natural resources valuable?

Read about the ways natural resources provide energy.

Natural Resources and Energy

Click! It's that easy to turn on a lamp. But where does that electricity come from? It probably comes from a power plant far away. That plant most likely burns coal to create electricity. Coal comes from deep within the earth. Coal is a natural **resource**.

Natural resources are nature's gifts, the riches that exist in the natural world. They include metals and minerals, plants, soil, and animals in the wild. They also include the things that are a **necessity** for all life—water, air, and sunlight.

We use natural resources to get or make energy. Energy makes things work. It runs our cars, computers, telephones, and machines. Natural resources are our energy sources.

There are two types of energy sources. Renewable sources do not run out. Sunlight and wind are examples of renewable energy. In contrast, nonrenewable sources can be used up. Coal, natural gas, and oil are nonrenewable. Only **limited** amounts of them exist. Nuclear energy is also nonrenewable. This type of energy uses a metal called uranium. Amounts of this metal are also limited.

Cooling towers at a nuclear facility

A natural gas pipeline

Text Evidence

1 Expand Vocabulary

A **resource** is something that is useful. Reread the first paragraph. **Circle** the name of one natural *resource*. What is it used to create?

_____

2 Comprehension
Author's Point of View

Underline words and phrases that are clues to what the author thinks about natural resources. What is the author's point of view?

_____

_____

3 Expand Vocabulary

When something is **limited**, there is a certain amount of it. The amount cannot change. List energy sources that have *limited* amounts.

_____

245

Text Evidence

1 Organization (A)(C)(T)

Reread the text under the heading "Challenges and Problems." What is the main idea of this section?

_____

_____

2 Comprehension
Author's Point of View

Reread the last two paragraphs. **Underline** clues to the author's position on using nonrenewable energy sources. What is the author's point of view?

_____

_____

3 Expand Vocabulary

When something is **global**, it has to do with the whole world. **Circle** details that help you understand the meaning of *global*.

People have always used renewable energy. Wind has been used to move ships. Wood was burned to cook food. Then, about 150 years ago, new machines needed more energy. People had to come up with new ways to get energy from natural resources. From the 19th century on, most of that energy has come from nonrenewable sources.

Challenges and Problems

Meeting our demand for more energy has not been easy. Supplies of coal, natural gas, oil, and uranium are deep underground. They must be found. They must be removed from the ground. These natural resources also have to be processed so they can be used. For example, oil is processed to become gasoline.

Although nonrenewable energy sources have met our needs, using them can cause problems. They can run out. They can also pollute, or harm, the environment. Some scientists say that gases from burning coal have heated up Earth's atmosphere. They say that this **global** warming will **affect** our climate so much that **glaciers** will melt and sea levels will rise.

Using nonrenewable sources can cause harm in other ways. Oil from spills often **seeps** into the ocean. Getting natural gas from the ground can also ruin an area. Nuclear energy creates dangerous waste.

U.S. Energy Use from **1949–2010**

Types of Energy, Percentage of Energy Used by Year (approximate)

SOURCE OF ENERGY	1949	1969	1989	2010
Nonrenewable Energy	91%	94%	92%	92%
Renewable Energy	9%	6%	8%	8%

We must find ways to meet our energy challenges. One way is to use renewable sources of energy. However, energy from renewable sources can be hard to make available everywhere. Bringing this type of energy to homes and businesses can also cost a lot.

When solar panels are placed on a roof, they help provide heat and electricity.

Solutions for the Future

Using the sun's energy shows promise. Solar panels can **absorb**, or take in, the sun's energy. They can be used to heat buildings. But solar energy can only be gotten during the day. Earth turns on its axis and **circulates** in a yearly **cycle** around the sun. So the amount of daylight changes in certain places. The sun's energy is sometimes less available. We will have to think of new ways we can get and store energy from the sun and other renewable sources.

We also can use nonrenewable energy more wisely. Government and businesses can work on **reducing** pollution. Moreover, people can try to **conserve**, or save, energy. We can turn off lights and TVs when we are not using them. These small efforts can add up and change how we use energy in the future.

Oil rigs, which are used for drilling oil, are often found in seas away from the shore.

(bkgd) morkeman/Vetta/Getty Images; (t) David J. Green/Alamy

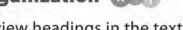

Text Evidence

1 Comprehension
Author's Point of View

Underline clues to the author's position on using the sun's energy. What is the author's point of view?

_____

_____

2 Expand Vocabulary

Reducing means making something less or smaller. List two things the author says people can *reduce*.

_____

_____

3 Organization A C T

Review headings in the text. How does the author organize ideas?

_____

_____

Respond to Reading

Discuss Work with a partner. Read the questions about "Power from Nature." Use the discussion starters to answer the questions. Write the page numbers to show where you found text evidence.

 Questions   **Discussion Starters**    **Text Evidence**

1 Why are water, air, and sunlight important natural resources?

- ▶ Water, air, and sunlight are important because…
- ▶ Another reason they are important is because they can…

Page(s): _____

2 How do people use natural resources?

- ▶ One way people use natural resources is to…
- ▶ Natural resources help us…
- ▶ I read that…

Page(s): _____

3 Why is the amount of natural resources we use important?

- ▶ The amount of natural resources we use is important because…
- ▶ The amounts of coal, natural gas, and oil are important because…
- ▶ I know this because I read that…

Page(s): _____

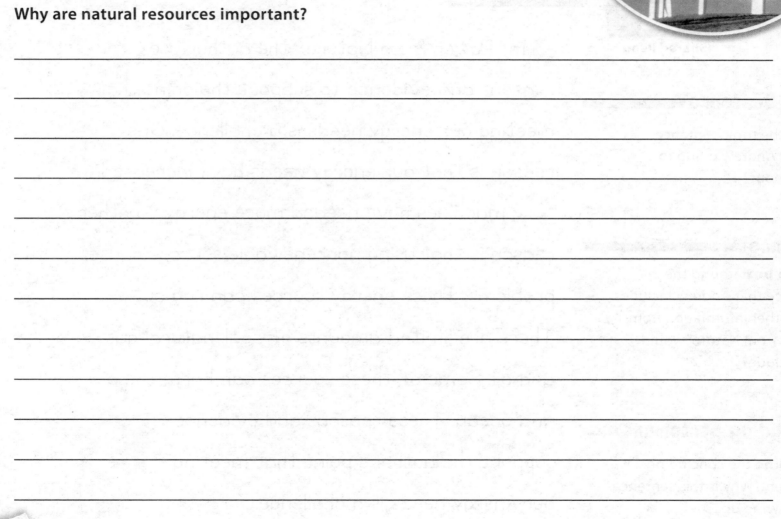

Write Review your notes about "Power from Nature." Then write your answer to the question below. Use text evidence to support your answer.

Why are natural resources important?

_____

_____

_____

_____

_____

_____

_____

_____

_____

_____

_____

John A. Karachewski

Write About Reading

Shared Read

Author's Point of View Read Andrew's paragraph below about "Power from Nature." He analyzed how the author uses reasons and evidence.

Student Model

Topic Sentence

Circle the topic sentence. What is Andrew going to write about?

Evidence

Draw a box around the evidence that Andrew includes. What other information from "Power from Nature" would you include?

Concluding Statement

Underline the concluding statement. Why is this sentence a good wrap up?

In "Power from Nature," the author uses reasons and evidence to support the point that meeting our energy needs is a challenge. One reason is that our energy needs have increased. New machines have needed more energy. Another reason is that using nonrenewable sources causes problems. These energy sources can run out. There are limited amounts of coal, natural gas, and oil. Some of these sources can harm the air and ocean. These reasons and evidence support the author's point that meeting our energy needs is a challenge.

Leveled Reader

Write an Analysis   **Author's Point of View**   Write a paragraph about "The Delta." Review Chapter 1. Tell how the author uses reasons and evidence.

_____

_____

_____

_____

_____

_____

_____

_____

_____

_____

_____

_____

Topic Sentence

☐ Include the title of the text you read.

☐ Tell whether the author uses reasons and evidence to support a point.

☐ Include the author's point of view.

Evidence

☐ Include reasons the author gives.

☐ Include text evidence that supports the author's point.

Concluding Statement

☐ Restate how the author uses reasons and evidence to support a point.

Talk About It

Weekly Concept Express Yourself

Essential Question

How do you express something that is important to you?

Go Digital!

252

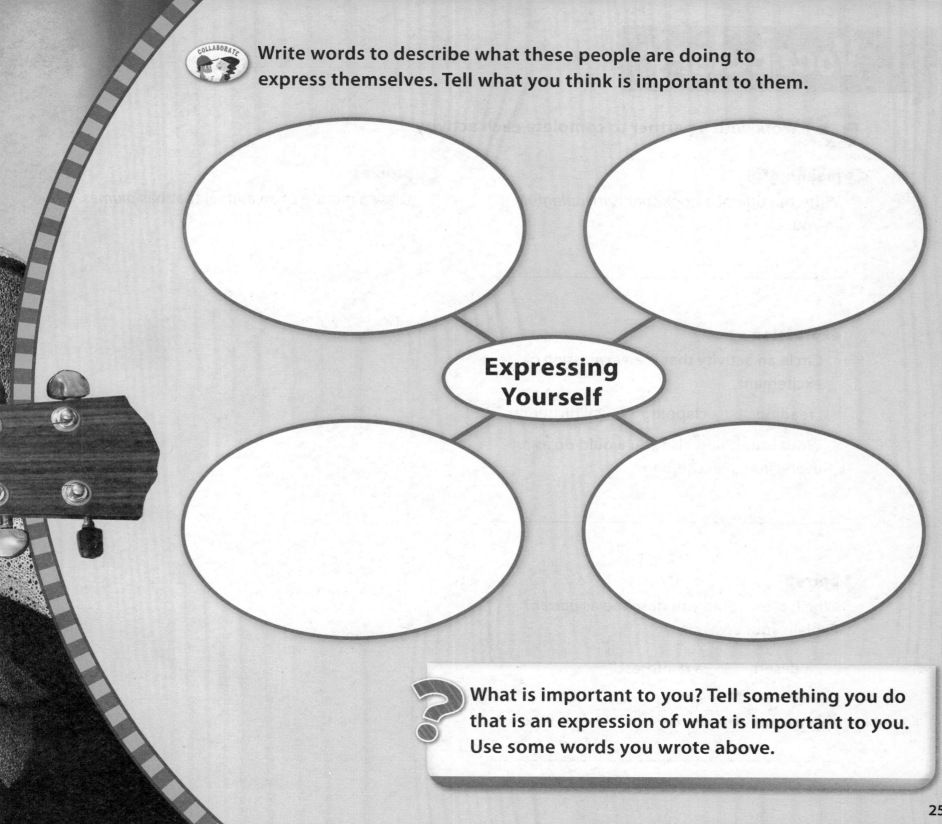

Write words to describe what these people are doing to express themselves. Tell what you think is important to them.

Expressing Yourself

What is important to you? Tell something you do that is an expression of what is important to you. Use some words you wrote above.

Vocabulary

 Work with a partner to complete each activity.

1 meaningful

Write the title of a book that is *meaningful* to you.

_____

2 expression

▶ Circle an activity that is an *expression* of excitement.

   reading   clapping   whispering

▶ Write something else you would do as an *expression* of excitement.

_____

3 barren

Which area would you describe as *barren*? Explain your answer.

   a desert   a rainforest

_____

_____

4 plumes

Draw a picture of an animal that has *plumes*.

Read the poem. Work with a partner to complete each activity.

FREE TIME

I go fast on my skateboard.
Push and pump and ride.

The pavement is my playmate.
Hop and stop and glide.

I feel free as I travel.
Turn and twist and slide.

No bumps can bother me.
Leap and lift and fly.

5 lyric

Lyric poetry describes a poet's feelings about something. **Draw a box** around a line in "Free Time" that shows a strong feeling.

6 alliteration

Alliteration is when two or more words in a line begin with the same consonant sound. **Circle** an example of alliteration in "Free Time."

7 meter

A poem's *meter* is the pattern of stressed and unstressed syllables in each line. How many stressed syllables are there in the second line?

_____

8 stanza

A *stanza* is a group of lines in a poem. How many stanzas are in "Free Time"?

_____

My Notes

Use this page to take notes during your first read of the poems.

Shared Read | Genre • Poetry

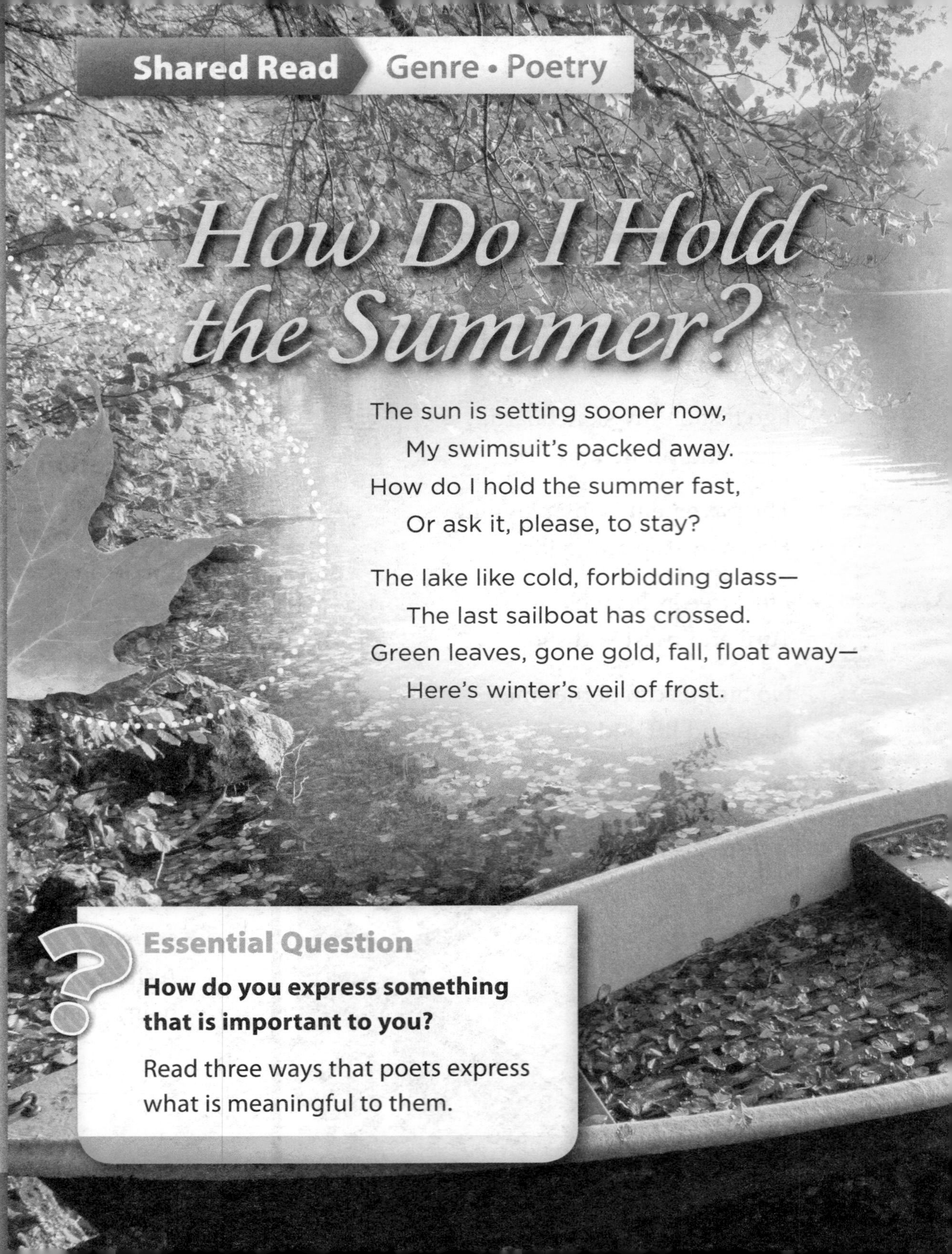

How Do I Hold the Summer?

The sun is setting sooner now,
    My swimsuit's packed away.
How do I hold the summer fast,
    Or ask it, please, to stay?

The lake like cold, forbidding glass—
    The last sailboat has crossed.
Green leaves, gone gold, fall, float away—
    Here's winter's veil of frost.

Essential Question

How do you express something that is important to you?

Read three ways that poets express what is meaningful to them.

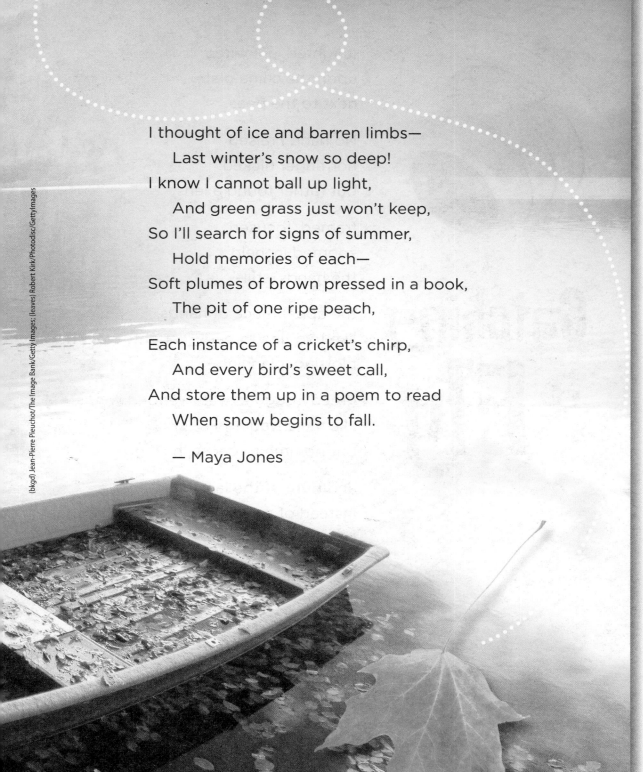

I thought of ice and barren limbs—
    Last winter's snow so deep!
I know I cannot ball up light,
    And green grass just won't keep,
So I'll search for signs of summer,
    Hold memories of each—
Soft plumes of brown pressed in a book,
    The pit of one ripe peach,

Each instance of a cricket's chirp,
    And every bird's sweet call,
And store them up in a poem to read
    When snow begins to fall.

    — Maya Jones

Text Evidence

❶ Literary Elements
Stanza and Meter

Circle two lines in the first stanza that have the same meter. How are details in the first two stanzas alike?

_____

_____

❷ Connection of Ideas Ⓐ Ⓒ Ⓣ

Draw a box around details that describe memories of summer. Do these details express a positive or negative feeling about summer?

_____

_____

❸ Comprehension
Theme

Underline key details. What is the speaker's main message about how to hold onto memories?

_____

_____

257

Text Evidence

① Connection of Ideas ACT

Review the title and photographs. Reread the first stanza. What does "it" refer to? **Circle** text evidence.

_____

② Literary Elements
Metaphor

Draw a box around a metaphor. What two things are compared?

_____

_____

③ Comprehension
Theme

Underline key details. What is the poem's main message about how to treat other living things?

_____

_____

_____

Catching a Fly

It lighted, uninvited
upon the china plate
next to the peas.

No hand I raised
nor finger flicked
but rather found a lens

framed, focused,
zoomed in, held
the hands, still—

the appearance of hands,
like two fine threads, caught
plotting, planning—

greedy goggle eyes, webbed wings
like me, invading—
but no time to pause, he'd go—

and right at the last
instead of a swat,
I snapped!

— Ken Kines

WHEN I DANCE

Always wanna break out,
    use my arms and legs
        to shout!

On any dark day
    that doesn't go
        exactly my way—

I bust a move,
    get a groove,
        feet feel the ground—

That slap's
    the only sound
        slap, pound

my body needs to charge,
    I play my tracks,
        I make it large

to take myself away!
    Nothing else
        I need to say.

— T.C. Arcaro

Text Evidence

❶ Literary Elements
Alliteration

Reread the first three stanzas.
Underline examples of alliteration.

❷ Connection of Ideas Ⓐ Ⓒ Ⓣ

What do details in the fourth stanza
tell you about the speaker's way of
dancing?

_____

_____

_____

❸ Comprehension
Theme

Circle key details. What is the
speaker's main message about
dancing?

_____

_____

_____

Respond to Reading

 COLLABORATE

 **Discuss** Work with a partner. Read the questions about the poems "How Do I Hold the Summer?", "Catching a Fly," and "When I Dance." Use the discussion starters to answer the questions. Write the page numbers where you found text evidence.

❓ Questions

💬 Discussion Starters

 **🔍 Text Evidence**

	Questions	Discussion Starters	Text Evidence
1	In "How Do I Hold the Summer?" what does the speaker do to show that summer is important?	► The speaker shows that summer is important by… ► I can tell the speaker thinks this is important because…	Page(s): _____
2	In "Catching a Fly," what does the speaker do to show that a fly can be important?	► The speaker showed that a fly is important by… ► I know this because I read that…	Page(s): _____
3	In "When I Dance," what does the speaker do to show that feeling good is important?	► The speaker shows that feeling good is important by… ► I can tell the speaker thinks this is important because… ► I noticed that…	Page(s): _____

Write Review your notes about the poems "How Do I Hold the Summer?", "Catching a Fly", and "When I Dance." Then write your answer to the question below. Use text evidence to support your answer.

How did the speaker of each poem express what is important?

_____

_____

_____

_____

_____

_____

_____

_____

_____

_____

Write About Reading

Shared Read

Student Model

Topic Sentence

Circle the topic sentence. What is Ben going to write about?

Evidence

Draw a box around the evidence that Ben includes. What other details from the poem would you include?

Concluding Statement

Underline the concluding statement. Why is this sentence a good wrap up?

In "How Do I Hold the Summer?" the poet uses sensory language to show the change in seasons. The lake is "like cold, forbidding glass." This helps me imagine how the lake would feel and look. "Green leaves, gone gold, fall, float away" is another example of sensory language. I can picture the color of the leaves and how they move. The words "a cricket's chirp, and every bird's sweet call" help me imagine the sounds of summer. All of these details help me imagine the change in seasons.

262

Leveled Reader

Write an Analysis ▸ Genre Write a paragraph about "Tell Me the Old, Old Stories." Review Chapter 2. Tell how the author uses sensory language to show Manuel's experience at his family's party.

_____

_____

_____

_____

_____

_____

_____

_____

_____

_____

_____

Topic Sentence

- ☐ Include the title of the text you read.

- ☐ Tell whether the author uses sensory language to show Manuel's experience at his family's party.

Evidence

- ☐ Include examples of sensory language.

- ☐ Explain why sensory language helped you imagine the experience.

Concluding Statement

- ☐ Restate how the author uses sensory language.

What's Next?

The Big Idea

In what ways can things change?

Talk About It

Weekly Concept New Perspectives

Essential Question

What experiences can change the way you see yourself and the world around you?

Go Digital!

266

Look at the photograph. Tell about the girl's experience. Then write words that describe her view of the world.

New Perspectives

 Describe an experience that made you see yourself or the world in a new way. Use some words above.

Vocabulary

 Work with a partner to complete each activity.

1 **genius**

Circle two words you would use to describe a *genius*.

smart   clumsy   skilled

2 **focused**

Write one way you stay *focused* when you are doing your homework.

_____

_____

3 **stunned**

The word *shocked* is a synonym for *stunned*. Circle two more synonyms for *stunned*.

bored   amazed   surprised

4 **superb**

Write the name of a person who you think is a *superb* athlete.

_____

5 **disdain**

Think of a type of music or a sound you don't like to hear. Show how you would express *disdain* for it. Use your face and hands.

6 **prospect**

Describe how you would feel about the *prospect* of going to the beach. Explain your answer.

_____

_____

_____

7 **perspective**

Look to your right. Describe what you see from your *perspective*.

_____

_____

_____

8 transition

Think of an insect or other animal that goes through a *transition*. Draw a picture of the insect or animal before and after the *transition*.

High-Utility Words

▶ **Indefinite Pronouns**

Indefinite pronouns are pronouns that do not name the specific person, place, or thing they replace. Some examples are *all, few, most, anything,* and *everybody.*

Circle the indefinite pronouns in the passage.

Mia was new at school. She thought (most) of the kids in her class seemed nice, but she was too scared to talk to anybody. When some of the kids in the hall said hi, Mia was too shy to wave back. But she wanted to make friends. So Mia sat next to a few of the girls at lunch. Everyone was happy that Mia joined them. Mia was happy, too.

My Notes

Use this page to take notes during your first read of "Miguel in the Middle."

_____

_____

_____

_____

_____

_____

_____

_____

_____

_____

_____

_____

_____

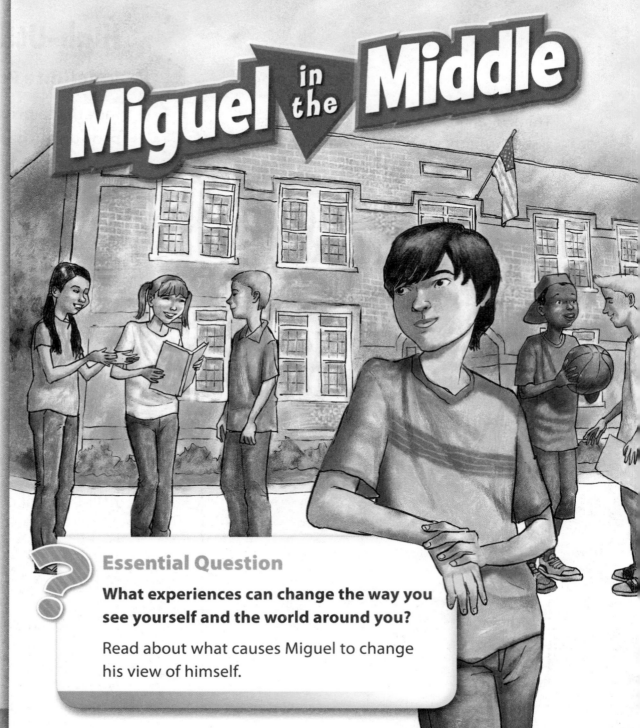

Miguel in the Middle

Essential Question

What experiences can change the way you see yourself and the world around you?

Read about what causes Miguel to change his view of himself.

For as long as I can remember, I've been in the middle. I'm the middle child in my family. And I've always sat in the middle of the classroom.

Luckily, I'm also in the middle of a large circle of friends. Most of them are classmates—at least they were until now. I started middle school in September, and the **transition** from elementary school caused some **painful** changes. All of my closest friends go to a different middle school because our school district changed. The only classmate I know from my old school is Jake. He's a **genius** in math. He knows everything about it, but since it's not my favorite subject, we never became friends. I've really missed my old friends.

Another big change is that I no longer sit in the middle of the classroom. I'm in the front row. Also, my new teachers give us more homework (especially in math). So you can imagine why my heart wasn't dancing when middle school began.

Rogerio Soud

TONIGHT'S MATH HOMEWORK

❶ Organization Ⓐ Ⓒ Ⓣ

What happens to Miguel in September?

_____

_____

❷ Expand Vocabulary

When something is **painful**, it causes a person to be upset. **Underline** a detail that shows that Miguel's experience is *painful*.

❸ Comprehension
Compare and Contrast

Draw a box around details that tell about Miguel's life in elementary school. **Circle** details about his life in middle school. How is Miguel's life different now?

_____

_____

_____

271

Text Evidence

1 Organization (A)(C)(T)

Reread the first paragraph. **Write "1"** next to the event that happens first. **Write "2"** next to the event that happens next. **Write "3"** next to the event that happens last.

2 Expand Vocabulary

When you **approach** someone, you walk up to them. Who did Miguel *approach*?

_____

_____

3 Comprehension
Compare and Contrast

Draw a box around details in the first paragraph that tell how Miguel is doing in math. **Circle** details that tell how Miguel is doing in math when he studies with Jake at home. How does Miguel change?

_____

_____

By the end of October, Jake and I had become good friends. It happened because I was having trouble with my math homework. I have a **disdain** for math—especially fractions. I hate them. To me, they are a foreign language, like reading Greek. So one day, I **approached** Jake when we were walking out of the school.

"Hey, Jake," I began, "I was wondering if you could—"

"Help you with the math homework?" he said, completing my sentence. "I'd be happy to help you, Miguel."

I was **stunned** because I wasn't sure until then if Jake even knew my name.

That night, Jake came over to my house to help me study. I must admit that he's a **superb** math teacher. He used slices of a pizza pie to explain the idea of eighths and sixteenths, and by the end of the night, I finally understood why eight-sixteenths is the same as one-half!

The next day in class, I was even able to answer a math problem our teacher put on the chalkboard!

I can't believe winter vacation is almost here! The school days have been flying by like a jet plane. I suppose it's because I'm a more **focused** student—especially in math—than I ever was before. Until this year, I always looked forward to the **prospect** of a school break. Now, I feel sad that I'll be away from school for two weeks.

The other day, the most amazing thing happened when our teacher gave us a math brainteaser. She asked, "If you wrote all the numbers from one to one hundred, how many times would you write a nine?"

Most of the students said ten, although some clever kids said eleven, because they **realized** that ninety-nine has two nines, not just one. But Jake and I were the only students who knew the correct answer—twenty! Everyone else forgot to count all the nineties.

I'm glad Jake and I get to hang out together during winter break. We're going to the Math Museum, and all my new friends from middle school will come, too. You see, even though I now have a completely different **perspective** on math, some things haven't changed. I'm still in the middle of a large circle of friends!

Rogerio Soud

Respond to Reading

Discuss Work with a partner. Use the discussion starters to answer the questions below about "Miguel in the Middle." Write the page numbers to show where you found text evidence.

? Questions	Discussion Starters	Text Evidence
1 What does Miguel think about middle school at the beginning of the story?	▶ At the beginning of the story, Miguel feels… ▶ Miguel first thinks that middle school is… ▶ I read that…	Page(s): ___
2 What does Miguel think about middle school at the end of the story?	▶ By the end of the story, Miguel feels… ▶ At the end, Miguel thinks that middle school is… ▶ I know this because I read…	Page(s): ___
3 What causes Miguel to change?	▶ Miguel changes because… ▶ Another reason Miguel changes is because… ▶ I noticed that…	Page(s): ___

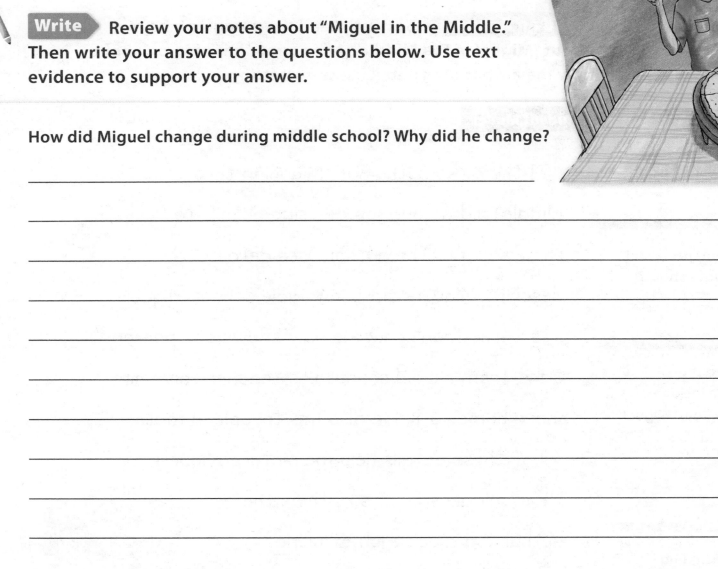

Write Review your notes about "Miguel in the Middle."
Then write your answer to the questions below. Use text
evidence to support your answer.

How did Miguel change during middle school? Why did he change?

_____

_____

_____

_____

_____

_____

_____

_____

_____

_____

Write About Reading

Shared Read

Read an Analysis Setting Read the paragraph below about "Miguel in the Middle." Anna wrote her opinion about how the author uses details to show setting.

Student Model

Topic Sentence

Circle the topic sentence. What is Anna going to write about?

Evidence

Draw a box around the evidence that Anna includes. What other details from "Miguel in the Middle" would you include?

Concluding Statement

Underline the concluding statement. Why is this sentence a good wrap up?

I think the author of "Miguel in the Middle" did a good job of using details to show setting. The author uses details to describe Miguel's class in middle school. Miguel sits in the front row. He only knows one person, Jake, from his old school. His teachers give him more homework. He also has trouble in math. All of these details help me picture Miguel's life in middle school, so I think the author did a good job of using details to show setting.

Leveled Reader

Write an Analysis ▶ **Setting** Write a paragraph about "King of the Board." Review Chapter 1. Tell your opinion about how the author uses details to show Bracefield Park.

_____

_____

_____

_____

_____

_____

_____

_____

_____

_____

_____

Topic Sentence

☐ Include the title of the text you read.

☐ State your opinion. Tell whether the author did a good job of using details to show setting.

Evidence

☐ Describe the setting using details from the story.

☐ Include only details that support your opinion.

Concluding Statement

☐ Restate your opinion. Wrap up the details that support your opinion.

Talk About It

Essential Question

How do shared experiences help people adapt to change?

Go Digital!

Write words to describe how people can help each other adapt to a change.

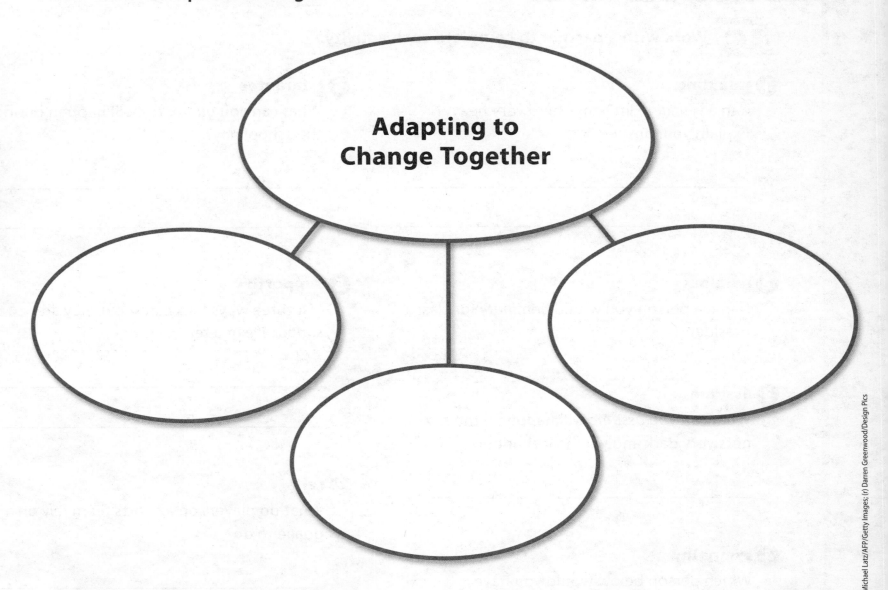

Adapting to Change Together

 Describe a change you have experienced. How did others help you? Use some of the words above.

Vocabulary

1 **weakling**

Can a *weakling* lift something very heavy? Explain your answer.

_____

_____

2 **nominate**

Name a person you would *nominate* for class president.

3 **assume**

What can you *assume* will happen if the sky gets very dark and you hear thunder?

_____

4 **sympathy**

Which person below would you have *sympathy* for? Circle your answer.

Kara lost a pet.

Jerome won a contest.

5 **guarantee**

What can you *guarantee* will happen during the school day?

_____

_____

6 **supportive**

List three ways fans can show they are *supportive* of a team.

_____

_____

7 **rely**

What do players on a sports team *rely* on a goalie to do?

_____

_____

280

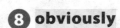

8 **obviously**

Draw a picture of an animal that is *obviously* bigger than another animal.

High-Utility Words

▶ **Compound Words**

A compound word is made up of two words.

Circle the compound words in the passage.

Dan helped his dad move boxes from the sidewalk into their new house. He walked inside and into the hallway.

"Let's find a place for the bookcase." Dad said. "Should it go in your bedroom?"

"What about somewhere downstairs?" Dan suggested. "You could put it in the living room where there is a fireplace!"

"Good idea!" Dad said. "I didn't want to carry it all the way upstairs anyway!"

My Notes

Use this page to take notes as you read "The Day the Rollets Got Their Moxie Back."

_____

_____

_____

_____

_____

_____

_____

_____

_____

_____

_____

_____

_____

_____

The Day the Rollets
Got Their Moxie Back

Essential Question

How do shared experiences help people adapt to change?

Read about how a family comes together during a period of great hardship in the United States.

Sometimes, the thing that gets you through hard times comes like a lightning bolt from the blue. That's what my brother's letter was like, traveling across the country from a work camp in Wyoming. It was 1937, and Ricky was working to create buildings for a state park as part of President Roosevelt's employment program. The program created jobs for young men, but it hadn't helped our dad find work yet.

I **imagined** Ricky looking up at snow-capped mountains, breathing in the smell of evergreens as he turned trees into lumber and lumber into buildings. It almost made an 11-year-old **weakling** like me want to become a lumberjack.

In our New York City apartment, the air smelled like meatloaf and cabbage. Dad sat in his chair, facing the window, **obviously** trying to catch the last rays of sunlight rather than turn on a light. My older sister Ruth and I compared our letters from Ricky. "Shirley, Ricky was in a talent show. He wore a grass skirt and did a hula dance while playing a little guitar!" Ruth reported. "I'll bet he was great!"

"It would be swell to have our own talent show!" I replied.

"Should I start sewing grass skirts?" Mom asked from the kitchen, which was just a corner of the room with a stove, sink, and icebox. "Come set the table. Dinner's almost ready."

Ron Mazellan

Text Evidence

❶ Genre Ⓐ Ⓒ Ⓣ
Historical Fiction

Reread the first paragraph. **Circle** details that tell you the story is set at a real time in history.

❷ Expand Vocabulary

When you **imagine** something, you picture it in your mind. **Underline** text that describes what the narrator *imagined*. Why did she *imagine* that?

_____

_____

❸ Genre Ⓐ Ⓒ Ⓣ
Historical Fiction

Historical fiction includes words that are typical of a certain time. Reread the last paragraph. **Draw a box** around the text that describes the kitchen. Which item in the kitchen has a different name today?

_____

283

Text Evidence

1 Expand Vocabulary

To **design** means to plan and create. **Draw a box** around clues to the meaning of *design*.

2 Comprehension
Compare and Contrast

Underline details that show Dad's feelings. **Underline** details that show Mom's feelings. How are Mom's and Dad's feelings different?

_____

_____

3 Comprehension
Compare and Contrast

Circle details that show how Ruth and the narrator feel about the talent show. How are they alike? How do they act differently?

_____

_____

_____

284

Dad stayed where he was, looking gloomy. "Any jobs in the paper?" Mom asked, her voice showing her **sympathy**. Dad shook his head no. He had been an artist for the theater, but most productions now had little cash. Dad drew show posters just to keep his skills sharp. He even **designed** posters showing Ruth and me in our costumes and named it "Rollet's Follies."

For dinner, Mom served a baked loaf of whatever ingredients she had. From the reddish color, I could **assume** it had beets in it. "I **guarantee** you'll like these beets," she said. "It's beet loaf, the meatless meat loaf," she sang as she served it.

Ruth fidgeted, excited about the idea of putting on a talent show. Though calm on the outside, inside I wanted to get started on it, too.

Over the next week, Ruth and I practiced a dance for our own talent show. Meanwhile, our parents began to worry about heating bills. Cold weather had set in. One Saturday, my father decided to grab some coffee at the local soup kitchen, hoping to hear news about any available jobs. Ruth and I begged to go along. Finally, he agreed.

Ron Mazellan

Most everyone in line outside the soup kitchen was bundled up to keep warm. Many had to **rely** on only thin layers to protect them from the cold. Like other men in line, Dad bowed his head as if in shame.

The line moved slowly. Ruth became bored. She began practicing her dance steps. I sang an upbeat tune to give her some music. Around us, people lifted their heads. Frowns turned to smiles. Folks began clapping along. Hearing the **supportive** response, Ruth danced with spirit.

"Those girls sure have moxie!" someone shouted.

"Why, they oughta be in pictures!" offered another.

"I'd **nominate** them for an Academy Award!" a woman called out.

"Those are my girls!" Dad said with pride.

Everyone burst into applause. For those short moments, the past didn't matter. We were all filled with hope for the future. I couldn't wait to write Ricky to tell him the news.

Text Evidence

❶ Comprehension
Compare and Contrast

Circle text that shows how people feel before Ruth starts to dance. **Circle** text that shows how people respond to Ruth's dancing. How do Ruth's actions affect others?

_____

_____

❷ Genre Ⓐ Ⓒ Ⓣ
Historical Fiction

Reread the dialogue. **Draw a box** around any expressions that people do not usually use today.

❸ Comprehension
Compare and Contrast

Review Dad's feelings before Ruth dances. **Underline** details that show how he feels at the end of the story. How has Dad changed?

_____

285

Respond to Reading

 **Discuss** Work with a partner. Use the discussion starters to answer the questions below about "The Day the Rollets Got Their Moxie Back." Write the page numbers to show where you found text evidence.

? Questions	**Discussion Starters**	**Text Evidence**
1 How do Ricky's letters affect the family?	▶ Ricky writes letters to his family because… ▶ When Ruth and Shirley read Ricky's letters, they feel… ▶ Ricky's letters give Ruth and Shirley the idea to…	Page(s): _____
2 What do Ruth and Shirley do to help Dad keep working?	▶ Ruth and Shirley help Dad keep working by… ▶ I read that Dad keeps his skills sharp by…	Page(s): _____
3 How do Ruth and Shirley make Dad feel better?	▶ At the soup kitchen, Dad first feels… ▶ At the soup kitchen, Ruth and Shirley decide to… ▶ Dad feels better because…	Page(s): _____

Mike Moran

286

Write Review your notes about "The Day the Rollets Got Their Moxie Back." Then write your answer to the question below. Use text evidence to support your answer.

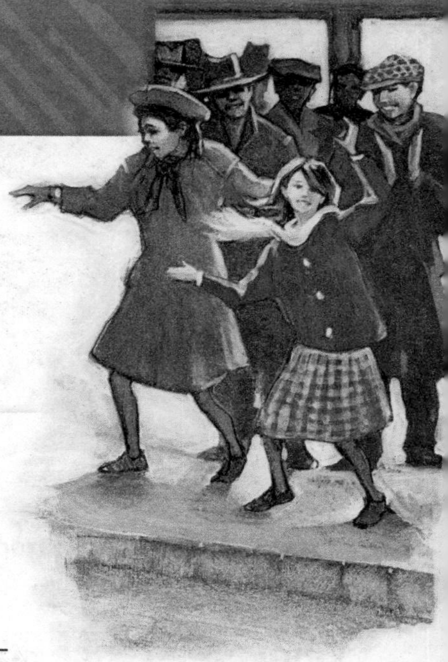

How do Ricky, Ruth, and Shirley help their family adapt to change?

Ron Mazellan

Write About Reading

Shared Read

Read an Analysis **Setting** Read Drew's paragraph below about "The Day the Rollets Got Their Moxie Back." He analyzed how the author uses details to show setting.

Student Model

Topic Sentence

Circle the topic sentence. What is Drew going to write about?

Evidence

Draw a box around the evidence that Drew includes. What other details from "The Day the Rollets Got Their Moxie Back" would you include?

Concluding Statement

Underline the concluding statement. Why is this sentence a good wrap up?

In "The Day the Rollets Got Their Moxie Back," the author uses many details that help me picture the setting. The author includes the year, 1937. The author also describes the apartment in New York City. It smells like cabbage and meatloaf. I can tell it is late in the day because Dad is trying to catch the last rays of sunlight. The kitchen is just a corner of the room with a stove, sink, and icebox. I can tell that the apartment must be very small. All of these details help me imagine what the Rollets' apartment looked and smelled like.

Ron Mazellan

288

Leveled Reader

Write an Analysis > Setting Write a paragraph about "The Picture Palace." Review Chapter 1. Tell how the author uses details to show setting.

_____

_____

_____

_____

_____

_____

_____

_____

_____

_____

_____

_____

Topic Sentence

☐ Include the title of the text you read.

☐ Tell whether the author uses details to show setting.

Evidence

☐ Tell the setting the author describes.

☐ Include details from the story that show the setting.

☐ Explain why the details help you picture the setting.

Concluding Statement

☐ Restate how the author uses details to show setting.

Talk About It

Essential Question

What changes in the environment affect living things?

Go Digital!

COLLABORATE Write words to describe the environment you see in the photograph. Tell how this environment affects the birds.

Changing Earth

? Describe a change you have seen in the environment. Use some of the words above.

(l) Fred Fred/Photononstop/Getty Images, (r) maxstock/Alamy

Vocabulary

 Work with a partner to complete each activity.

1 stability

Which has more *stability*?

bicycle   tricycle

2 decays

Describe what happens when a plant *decays*.

_____

_____

_____

3 impact

Circle the activity you think would have the greatest *impact* on a player's performance.

practice every day

watch a game on TV

4 gradual

Show how you would stack books in a *gradual* way.

5 noticeably

Circle two synonyms for *noticeably*.

clearly   slowly   obviously

6 atmosphere

Which animal can live in Earth's *atmosphere*? Explain your answer.

shark   bird   fish

_____

_____

_____

7 receding

When a wave is *receding* from the shore, which way is it going?

onto the sand   back out to the sea

292

8 variations

Draw two *variations* of a car.

High-Utility Words

▶ **Suffixes -*er* and -*est***

The suffix -*er* is added to an adjective to compare two things. The suffix -*est* is added to an adjective to compare more than two things.

Circle words that end with -*er*. **Underline** words that end with -*est*.

A blue whale is one of the <u>largest</u> animals. It is (bigger) than a shark. But the blue whale is not the fastest moving ocean animal. Blue whales are slower than sailfish, which swim at high speeds.

Blue whales migrate, but humpback whales travel greater distances. In fact, humpback whales have one of the longest migrations of all ocean animals!

Use this page to take notes during your first read of "Forests on Fire."

Forests on Fire

? Essential Question

What changes in the environment affect living things?

Read about the effects of forest fires on plants, animals, and people.

A few years ago, several red squirrels—an endangered species—were rescued from a wildfire that was destroying their habitat. Forest fires like that one can destroy thousands of acres of land and harm animals. Forest fires are a part of nature, so it is important for us to understand them. We need to know not only how to put these wildfires out, but why they happen.

Destructive and Productive

Like rainstorms, wildfires are a force of nature. However, unlike rainstorms, wildfires are almost always destructive. They cause damage to many plants and animals as they spread. Sometimes, they take human lives and homes as well.

Like big storms, wildfires are terrifying. On the other hand, wildfires that happen naturally can also produce, or make, necessary changes in **environments** such as forests or prairies. Just as rain helps new plants grow, wildfires can also allow new life to grow.

Benefits of Naturally Occurring Wildfires

A naturally occurring wildfire is a fire without any human cause. Three things must be present for a fire to burn. There must be fuel, such as dry grasses. There must be oxygen, which is a gas in the air, or **atmosphere**. There also needs to be a heat source to light the fuel. A natural wildfire is often sparked by a lightning strike. The danger of fire is highest when there has been little rain and plants are very dry.

Wildfires help to renew an environment. After vegetation **decays**, or rots, wildfires clear it away. Then new plant life can grow.

Text Evidence

❶ Purpose Ⓐ Ⓒ Ⓣ

Reread the first paragraph. What does the author want people to know about forest fires?

_____

_____

_____

_____

❷ Comprehension
Compare and Contrast

Reread "Destructive and Productive." **Draw a box** around three sentences that tell how wildfires and rainstorms are alike. **Underline** a sentence that tells how wildfires and rainstorms are different.

❸ Expand Vocabulary

An **environment** is the setting or area in which a person, plant, or animal lives. **Circle** two examples of _environments_ in the text.

Text Evidence

Open cone

New seedling

A young forest

Heat from a fire causes a black spruce tree cone to open and scatter seeds. Eventually, seedlings sprout, and a new forest will grow.

① Expand Vocabulary

To **depend** on something means to need or rely on it. **Underline** a clue to the meaning of *depend*.

② Comprehension

Compare and Contrast

Draw a box around text that describes different types of forests. How is a forest recently struck by fire different from one struck by fire twenty years ago?

_____

_____

_____

_____

_____

③ Expand Vocabulary

To **provide** means to supply or give something that is needed. **Circle** two things that forests *provide* for animals.

Fire also lets nutrients back into the soil. And by destroying leafy branches of large trees, fire allows sunlight to reach new growth on the forest floor.

This new plant life may be better adapted to fire than old plants. Some will develop roots, leaves, or bark that can resist fire. Other plants will **depend** on fire. They need fire to reproduce and grow.

Stability and Diversity

Another benefit of fire is that it brings **stability**. Fire kills plants that are not originally from a region, but may have started growing there. After fire, native plants can grow back.

Fire also ensures that an area has plants at different stages of growth. For example, a forest recently struck by fire will have new seedlings. Not far away, a forest struck by fire twenty years ago may have young trees. Nearby, there may be a forest of mature trees, untouched by fire for many years.

These **variations** in plant life **provide** food and habitats for different kinds of insects and animals. Insects find homes in burned-out trees. Seeds are food for sparrows. Squirrels and raccoons make their homes in mature trees. Foxes go after small forest animals.

The Human Factor

Although wildfires have benefits, they also are feared. In the past, our government tried to totally stop wildfires. This had a negative **impact** on the environment. The **gradual** buildup of decayed plants over many years provided more fuel to feed fires. Wildfires became **noticeably** fiercer.

Today, the government has ways to **manage** wildfires. One way is to limit fires before they burn out of control. Another way is to set small controlled fires. This reduces the amount of dry vegetation that is fuel for a fire. Hopefully, the danger of big fires is now **receding**.

Unfortunately, human carelessness also can start a fire. While a natural wildfire or a controlled fire can be good, this is not true of fires that result from human mistakes. These happen at times and places that may cause great harm to plant, animal, and human life. Fires cannot control themselves, so humans will always have to be careful about how best to handle them.

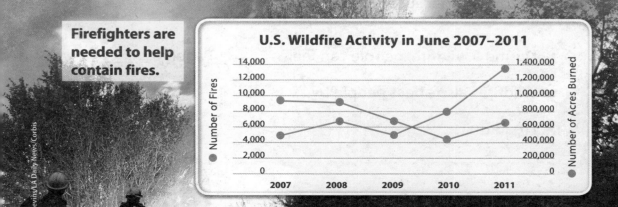

Firefighters are needed to help contain fires.

U.S. Wildfire Activity in June 2007–2011

Number of Fires: 14,000 / 12,000 / 10,000 / 8,000 / 6,000 / 4,000 / 2,000 / 0

Number of Acres Burned: 1,400,000 / 1,200,000 / 1,000,000 / 800,000 / 600,000 / 400,000 / 200,000 / 0

2007 2008 2009 2010 2011

©Gene Blevins/LA Daily News/Corbis

Text Evidence

① Comprehension
Compare and Contrast

Underline text that tells what the government did about wildfires in the past. **Underline** text that tells what the government does about wildfires today. How have the government's actions changed?

_____

_____

② Expand Vocabulary

When you **manage** something, you control or keep watch over it. **Draw a box** around two ways the government *manages* fires.

③ Purpose ⒶⒸⓉ

What does the author want people to do about wildfires? **Circle** text evidence.

_____

_____

297

Respond to Reading

Discuss Work with a partner. Use the discussion starters to answer the questions below about "Forests on Fire." Write the page numbers to show where you found text evidence.

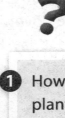

? Questions	Discussion Starters	Text Evidence
1 How do wildfires affect plants?	▶ During a wildfire, plants can be… ▶ After a wildfire, plants may… ▶ Another way plants are affected by wildfires is…	Page(s): _____
2 How do wildfires affect animals?	▶ During a wildfire, animals can be… ▶ After a wildfire, some animals can find… ▶ I know this because I read that…	Page(s): _____
3 How do wildfires affect people?	▶ During a wildfire, people can feel… ▶ Wildfires also affect people by… ▶ I read that…	Page(s): _____

Write Review your notes about "Forests on Fire." Then write your answer to the question below. Use text evidence to support your answer.

How do wildfires affect living things?

_____

_____

_____

_____

_____

_____

_____

_____

_____

_____

Write About Reading

Shared Read

Compare and Contrast Read Ian's paragraph below about "Forests on Fire." He analyzed how the author compares and contrasts information.

Student Model

In "Forests on Fire," the author compares and contrasts information to explain the effects of wildfires. Wildfires destroy land. Wildfires damage many plants and animals. The author compares these harmful effects to helpful effects of wildfires. Because wildfires clear away decayed plants, new plants can grow. Sunlight can reach new plants on the forest floor. By comparing and contrasting these details about wildfires, the author shows that wildfires can be both harmful and helpful.

Topic Sentence

Circle the topic sentence. What is Ian going to write about?

Evidence

Draw a box around the evidence that Ian includes. What other information from "Forests on Fire" would you include?

Concluding Statement

Underline the concluding statement. Why is this sentence a good wrap up?

Leveled Reader

Write an Analysis **Compare and Contrast** Write a paragraph about "Ocean Threats." Review Chapter 2. Tell how the author compares and contrasts information to explain the topic.

_____

_____

_____

_____

_____

_____

_____

_____

_____

_____

_____

Topic Sentence

☐ Include the title of the text.

☐ Tell whether the author compares and contrasts information.

☐ Include the topic of the chapter.

Evidence

☐ Include information in the text that the author compares and contrasts.

☐ Use only information that explains the topic.

Concluding Statement

☐ Restate how comparing and contrasting information explained the topic.

Talk About It

Weekly Concept Now We Know

Essential Question

How can scientific knowledge change over time?

Go Digital!

302

Write words to describe how people study Earth and space.
Write new discoveries you know about.

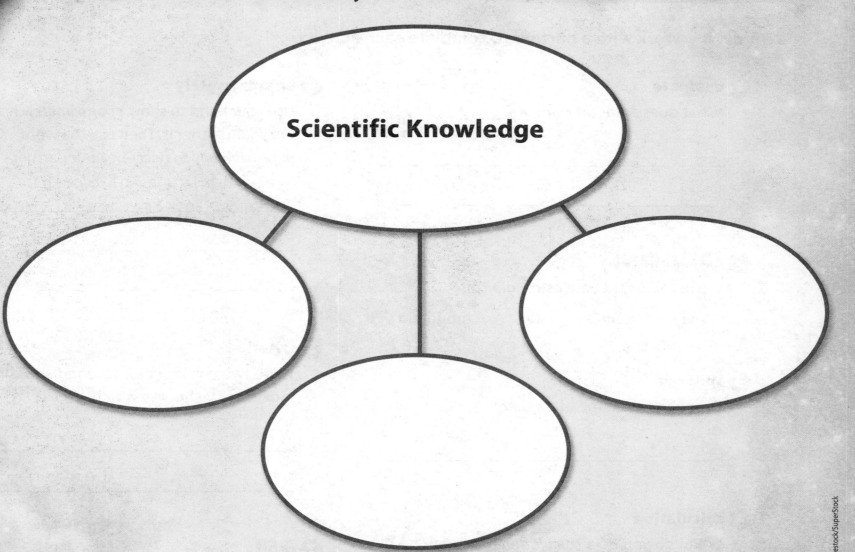

Scientific Knowledge

What do you want to know about space?
Describe how you would find out about it.
Use some words you wrote above.

Vocabulary

 Work with a partner to complete each activity.

1 **evaluate**

What does a doctor *evaluate*?

_____

_____

2 **astronomical**

Circle things that are *astronomical*.

    river   sun   star   mountain

3 **spheres**

Describe the shape of a *sphere*.

_____

4 **calculation**

When do you do a *calculation* in school?

_____

_____

5 **approximately**

Use your hand to show *approximately* how tall your partner is. Then use the word *approximately* to describe your partner's height.

_____

_____

_____

6 **criteria**

Write two *criteria* you use when choosing a movie or TV show to watch.

_____

_____

7 **orbit**

Show how you would *orbit* around the desk.

⑧ diameter

Draw a circle. Then draw a line to show its *diameter*.

High-Utility Words

▶ **Cause and Effect Signal Words**

Some words, such as *because, so, since,* and *as a result*, signal a cause-and-effect relationship.

Circle the words that signal a cause-and-effect relationship in the passage.

(Because) of a sudden storm, the scientists had to stop their research of the night sky. They pulled out umbrellas and packed up their equipment so it would not get wet. Since it started to rain hard, many of them found shelter in a building. As a result of the storm, the scientists plan to study the night sky tomorrow night. If the weather is good, they will be able to see the stars clearly.

My Notes

Use this page to take notes during your first read of "Changing Views of Earth."

_____

_____

_____

_____

_____

_____

_____

_____

_____

_____

_____

_____

_____

_____

CHANGING VIEWS OF EARTH

Essential Question

How can scientific knowledge change over time?

Read about how scientists were able to learn more about Earth over time.

From the Ground

No matter where you go, people like to talk about the weather. The weather forecast may provide the main **criteria** for planning activities. But where does all that weather information come from? The ability to predict Earth's weather patterns required many years of scientific innovation. We had to look up at the skies to learn more about Earth.

Long ago, humans mainly knew about Earth from what they saw and experienced. For example, they saw the rising Sun. They believed the Earth stayed in place and the Sun moved around it. People thought Earth was at the center of the solar system.

In the 1600s, an Italian named Galileo pointed a telescope toward the night sky. This new tool heightened his **vision**. He could see stars, planets, and other **spheres** in the sky more clearly. Each observation and **calculation** he made, such as distances between objects, led him to agree with another scientist's idea about the solar system. The scientist Copernicus had come up with a Sun-centered model. In this model, the Sun did not **orbit** the Earth. The Earth went around the Sun.

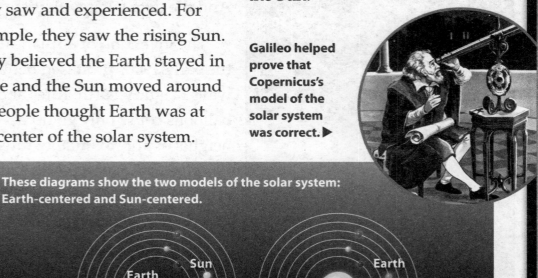

Galileo helped prove that Copernicus's model of the solar system was correct. ▶

These diagrams show the two models of the solar system: Earth-centered and Sun-centered.

Earth   Sun

Earth
Sun

❶ Expand Vocabulary

A person's **vision** is the ability to see. **Draw a box** around clues to the meaning of *vision*.

❷ Comprehension
Cause and Effect

Reread the third paragraph. **Circle** each cause. **Underline** each effect. What caused Galileo to agree with Copernicus?

_____

_____

❸ Connection of Ideas Ⓐ Ⓒ Ⓣ

Compare the two models of the solar system shown in the diagram. How are the models similar? How are they different?

_____

_____

_____

307

Text Evidence

❶ Expand Vocabulary

When something is **transported**, it is taken from one place to another. What did scientists use hot-air balloons to *transport*?

_____

_____

❷ Comprehension
Cause and Effect

Reread the last two paragraphs. **Circle** each cause. **Underline** each effect.

❸ Connection of Ideas ⒶⒸⓉ

Draw a box around three ways scientists sent devices into the atmosphere. Which way was the most successful? Give two details that support your answer.

_____

_____

_____

From the Sky

New tools like the telescope helped scientists better **evaluate**, or judge, others' ideas. Measuring tools like the thermometer gave scientists new information about weather patterns. However, people still got information from what they could see or measure from the ground. What if they could travel into the sky?

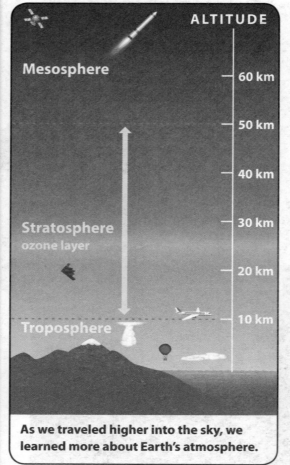

As we traveled higher into the sky, we learned more about Earth's atmosphere.

In the mid-1700s, scientists started to use kites to send measuring tools into the sky. Soon hot-air balloons also **transported** tools—and sometimes scientists— into the lower layers of the atmosphere.

However, the more scientists learned about the atmosphere, the higher they wanted to go. They also wanted to get information quickly and accurately. Although kites and balloons could go up high, they were hard to control. Wind sometimes blew them away. And the data went with them.

The invention of airplanes in the early 1900s promised better ways to study Earth. Kites and balloons could only go up to heights of **approximately** three kilometers. Airplanes could lift scientists to altitudes over five kilometers. Because airplanes had radio technology, data could be sent to scientists on the ground. But scientists dreamed of reaching ever higher.

From Space

Advances in air and space travel continued into the late twentieth century. Rockets could take satellites into orbit around Earth. From these heights, scientists could find out what the layers of the atmosphere were made up of. They could also measure the atmosphere's thinness. Both of these things affect weather. So scientists could make more accurate weather predictions.

NASA soon began sending more satellites into orbit. Some satellites looked at Earth. Others looked out into space. They **gathered astronomical** data. They collected information about the ages of planets and galaxies. Sensors and supercomputers accurately measured Earth's **diameter**. Because of all this technology, scientists were able to make better models of Earth's systems. They could even come up with new ideas about how climate might change over time.

Space missions continue to go farther from home. Views of our planet from space inspire awe, even in photographs. "With all the arguments . . . for going to the Moon," said astronaut Joseph Allen, "no one suggested that we should do it to look at the Earth. But that may in fact be the most important reason."

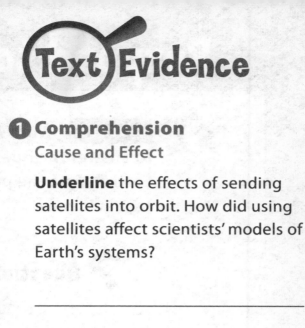

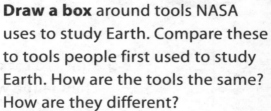
Satellites in orbit last for a limited number of years and then must be replaced.

Text Evidence

❶ Comprehension
Cause and Effect

Underline the effects of sending satellites into orbit. How did using satellites affect scientists' models of Earth's systems?

_____

_____

❷ Expand Vocabulary

To **gather** means to get or collect. **Circle** a word that has almost the same meaning as *gathered*.

❸ Connection of Ideas (A)(C)(T)

Draw a box around tools NASA uses to study Earth. Compare these to tools people first used to study Earth. How are the tools the same? How are they different?

_____

_____

_____

Respond to Reading

 Discuss Work with a partner. Use the discussion starters to answer the questions below about "Changing Views of Earth." Write the page numbers to show where you found text evidence.

? Questions	**Discussion Starters**	**Text Evidence**
1 How did kites and hot-air balloons change the way scientists study Earth?	► Scientists used kites and hot-air balloons to… ► Kites and hot-air balloons could go… ► I know this because I read that…	Page(s): _____
2 How did airplanes change the way scientists study Earth?	► Airplanes changed the way scientists study Earth because they could… ► Another way airplanes help scientists study Earth is by…	Page(s): _____
3 How did rockets change the way scientists study Earth?	► Rockets changed the ways scientists study Earth because they could… ► I know rockets are helpful for studying Earth because I read that…	Page(s): _____

Mike Moran

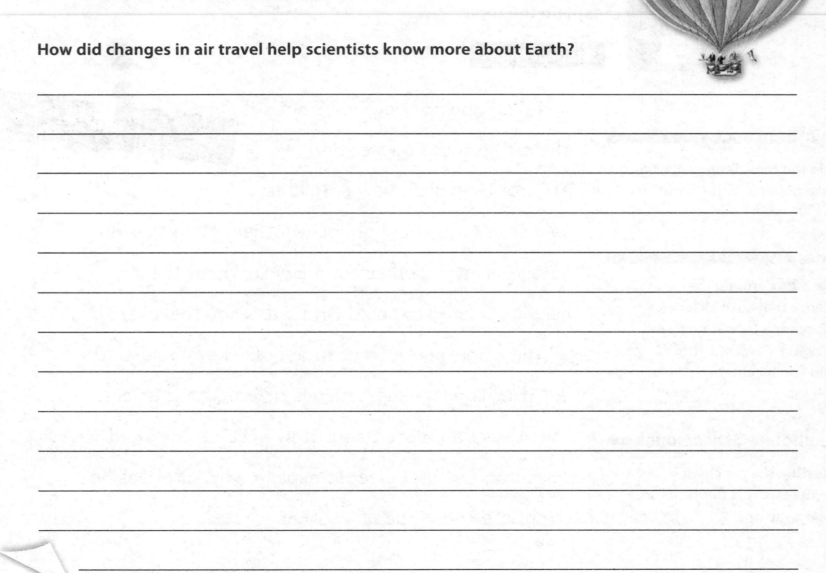

Write ▶ Review your notes about "Changing Views of Earth." Then write your answer to the question below. Use text evidence to support your answer.

How did changes in air travel help scientists know more about Earth?

_____

_____

_____

_____

_____

_____

_____

_____

_____

_____

Write About Reading

Shared Read

Read an Analysis Cause and Effect **Read Luke's paragraph below about "Changing Views of Earth." He analyzed how the author uses causes and effects to explain the topic.**

Student Model

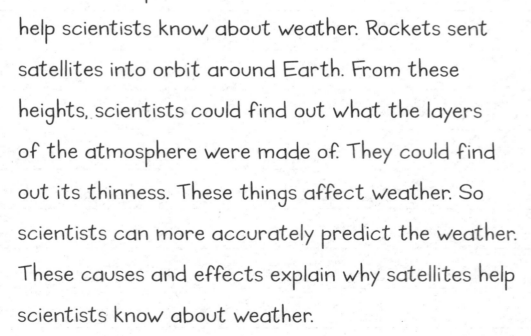

In "Changing Views of Earth," the author uses causes and effects to explain why satellites help scientists know about weather. Rockets sent satellites into orbit around Earth. From these heights, scientists could find out what the layers of the atmosphere were made of. They could find out its thinness. These things affect weather. So scientists can more accurately predict the weather. These causes and effects explain why satellites help scientists know about weather.

Topic Sentence

Circle the topic sentence. What is Luke going to write about?

Evidence

Draw a box around the evidence that Luke includes. What other information from "Changing Views of Earth" would you include?

Concluding Statement

Underline the concluding statement. Why is this sentence a good wrap up?

Leveled Reader

Write an Analysis **Cause and Effect** Write a paragraph about "Mars." Review Chapter 1. Tell how the author uses causes and effects to explain discoveries about Mars.

_____

_____

_____

_____

_____

_____

_____

_____

_____

_____

_____

Topic Sentence

☐ Include the title of the text you read.

☐ Tell whether the author uses causes and effects to explain the topic.

Evidence

☐ Tell what caused astronomers to know more about Mars.

☐ Describe the effects of using a telescope.

☐ Include only causes and effects that explain the topic.

Concluding Statement

☐ Restate how the author uses causes and effects to explain the topic.

313

Talk About It

Essential Question

How do natural events and human activities affect the environment?

Go Digital!

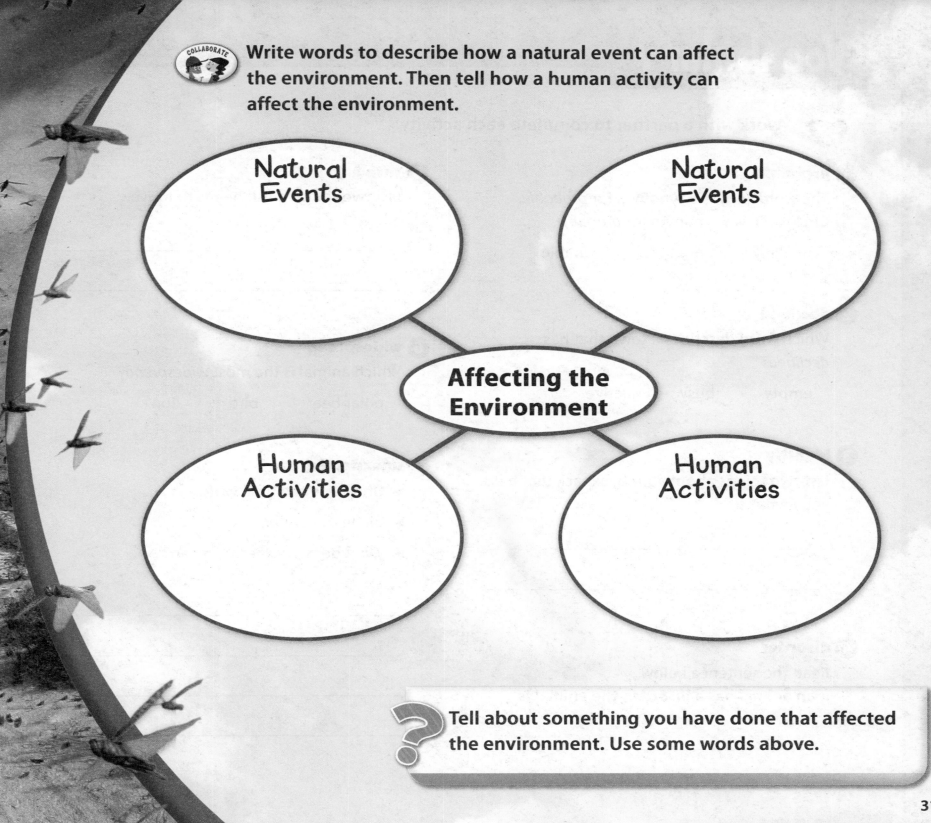

Write words to describe how a natural event can affect the environment. Then tell how a human activity can affect the environment.

Natural Events

Natural Events

Affecting the Environment

Human Activities

Human Activities

Tell about something you have done that affected the environment. Use some words above.

Vocabulary

 Work with a partner to complete each activity.

1 probable

The word *likely* is a synonym for *probable*.
Circle another synonym for *probable*.

   unlikely   possible   unable

2 declined

Which word describes a town that has *declined*?

   empty   busy   active

3 identify

List two things about your backpack that help you *identify* it.

_____

_____

4 disorder

Read the sentence below.
If an animal has a *disorder*, the animal is

_____

5 thrive

List two things a fish needs to *thrive*.

_____

_____

6 widespread

Which animal is the most *widespread*?

   polar bear   bird   lion

7 unexpected

▶ Underline the base word.

▶ Circle the prefix.

▶ What does *unexpected* mean?

_____

_____

_____

_____

8 agricultural

Draw a picture of an *agricultural* tool.

High-Utility Words

▶ **Suffix -ful**

The suffix *-ful* means "having" or "full of." For example, the word *hopeful* means "full of hope."

Circle words that end *-ful* in the passage.

Jen's dog Bo is big and (powerful.) But Bo is also very playful. No one is fearful of Bo. When Jen takes Bo to the park, they play catch. Jen is careful not to throw the ball too high. Bo can catch the ball in his mouth. Bo is skillful at catching the ball in the air.

317

My Notes

Use this page to take notes during your first read of "Should Plants and Animals from Other Places Live Here?"

_____

_____

_____

_____

_____

_____

_____

_____

_____

_____

_____

_____

? Essential Question

How do natural events and human activities affect the environment?

Read two different views on the arrival of new species into the United States.

It's hard to imagine life without oranges and chickens, which are examples of nonnative species.

Should Plants and Animals from Other Places Live Here?

New Arrivals Welcome

Nonnative species are good to have around!

Did you know that some plants and animals in the United States come from other places? These plants and animals are called *nonnative* species. Some are called *invasive* when they harm the environment, our health, or businesses. Some can take over a **widespread** area. The **population**, or number, of some native species has **declined** because of invasive species. But good things come from some nonnative species, too.

In Florida, for example, about 2,000 species of plants and animals are not from the area, including oranges and chickens, and sugarcane. These species are good for business. In fact, 90 percent of farm sales come from the sale of nonnative species.

Nonnative species can help to control pests that harm crops. Some scientists **identify** a pest's natural enemy, such as an insect, and bring it to farms to kill pests. Stopping pests is a good thing. Plus, this way of controlling a pest reduces the use of pesticides. For example, Vedalia beetles were brought here from Australia to eat insects that kill citrus fruit. The beetles were successful and farmers stayed in business!

Many dogs and cats come from other places, too. Labrador retrievers and Siamese cats are just two examples. Nonnative species like these surely make our lives better!

Text Evidence

1 Comprehension
Author's Point of View

Underline opinion words and phrases. Does the author have a positive or negative point of view toward nonnative species?

_____

2 Expand Vocabulary

The **population** of a place is the total number of living things in an area. **Circle** a clue to the meaning of the word in the first paragraph.

3 Purpose A C T

Draw a box around the sentences that tell about Vedalia beetles. What is the author's purpose in telling about this species?

_____

_____

_____

319

Text Evidence

1 Comprehension

Author's Point of View

Underline opinion words and phrases. Does the author have a positive or negative point of view toward nonnative species?

_____

_____

2 Expand Vocabulary

When something is **threatening,** it is likely the results will not be good. **Circle** text that tells what pythons are _threatening_ to do.

3 Purpose ACT

Draw a box around the costs to fix the damage from nonnative species. What is the author's purpose of including this fact?

_____

_____

_____

A Growing Problem

Foreign plants and animals threaten our country.

Visitors to the Florida Everglades expect to see alligators, not pythons. These huge snakes are from Asia. But about 150,000 pythons are crawling through the Everglades. The **probable** reason they are there is that people who kept pythons as pets dumped them in the wild. No one knows for sure. Now the pythons are a problem, **threatening** to reduce the population of native species.

Although some nonnative species are useful, others are harmful. It costs the U.S. $137 billion each year to fix the damage these species cause to the environment. Problems start when a species becomes invasive. For example, Asian carp was brought here and was able to **thrive** in the Mississippi River. Now the fish is a danger to the Great Lakes ecosystem. Because of its large appetite, the number of native fish has gone down.

Some germs are also a problem. A flu virus came to the U.S. carried by birds. This germ can cause a lung **disorder**, or illness, in people.

Agricultural experts sometimes bring in nonnative species to help the environment. But this can create **unexpected** problems. A hundred years ago, melaleuca trees were brought to Florida from Australia to preserve swampy areas. Now millions of these trees crowd out endangered native plants.

The facts lead to one conclusion: We must remove invasive species and keep new ones from arriving.

Nonnative Species: Benefits and Costs

Over the years, about 50,000 nonnative species have entered the U.S. The chart shows the helpful and harmful effects of four nonnative species.

SPECIES	NATIVE LAND	ENTERED THE U.S.	HELPFUL EFFECTS	HARMFUL EFFECTS
Horse	Europe	Early 1500s, on purpose	Used for work, moving people, fun	Made large-scale wars possible
Kudzu	Asia	Early 1800s, on purpose	Stops soil erosion	Crowds out native plants
Olives	Middle East and Europe	Early 1700s (farming began in 1800s), on purpose	Food source, cooking oil, important to California businesses	Only helps businesses in the few places where it can grow.
Mediterranean Fruit Fly	Africa	1929 (first recorded), accidentally	Food source for spiders	Destroys 400 species of plants, including citrus and vegetable crops

Although this community is trying to control invasive melaleuca plants, these plants have taken over the marsh.

CAUTION
MELALEUCA CONTROL PROJECT IN MARSH AREAS

(bkgd) Jeff Greenberg/Alamy; (t to b) Ingram Publishing; Matt Meadows/Peter Arnold/Getty Images; Emilio Simion/Photodisc/Getty Images; Jack Dykinga/USDA

Text Evidence

1 Purpose ⒶⒸⓉ

Draw a box around the sentence that tells the purpose of the chart.

2 Comprehension
Author's Point of View

Think about the author's point of view in "New Arrivals Welcome." **Circle** details in the chart that support the point that nonnative species are good for businesses.

3 Comprehension
Author's Point of View

Think about the author's point of view in "A Growing Problem." **Underline** details in the chart that support the point that nonnative species threaten native plants. What other information on this page supports this point of view?

_____

_____

_____

Respond to Reading

Discuss Work with a partner. Use the discussion starters to answer the questions below about "Should Plants and Animals from Other Places Live Here?" Write the page numbers where you found text evidence.

 Questions   **Discussion Starters**    **Text Evidence**

1 How did bringing Vedalia beetles to the U.S. affect other living things?	▶ One effect of bringing Vedalia beetles to the U.S. was… ▶ Another effect of bringing Vedalia beetles to the U.S. was… ▶ I know this because I read that…	Page(s): _____
2 How did bringing Asian carp to the U.S. affect the environment?	▶ After Asian carp was brought to the U.S., the fish… ▶ Another effect of having Asian carp brought to the U.S. is…	Page(s): _____
3 How does the nonnative plant kudzu affect the environment?	▶ Kudzu can be helpful to the environment by… ▶ One way kudzu is harmful is that… ▶ I read that…	Page(s): _____

Write Review your notes about "Should Plants and Animals from Other Places Live Here?" Then write your answer to the question below. Use text evidence to support your answer.

How does bringing nonnative species into the U.S. affect the environment?

_____

_____

_____

_____

_____

_____

_____

_____

_____

Write About Reading

Shared Read

Read an Analysis **Point of View** Read Noah's paragraph below about "Should Plants and Animals From Other Places Live Here?" Noah told how the author uses reasons and evidence to support a position on a topic.

Student Model

Topic Sentence

Circle the topic sentence. What is Noah going to write about?

Evidence

Draw a box around the evidence that Noah includes. What other information from "A Growing Problem" would you include?

Concluding Statement

Underline the concluding statement. Why is this sentence a good wrap up?

In "A Growing Problem," the author uses reasons and evidence to support the position that nonnative species are a problem. One reason is that nonnative species can threaten populations of native species. Pythons, Asian carp, and melaleuca trees all can affect populations of native species. Another reason is that nonnative species damage the environment. It costs the U.S. $137 billion each year to fix the damage. These reasons and evidence support the author's position that nonnative species are a problem.

Leveled Reader

Write an Analysis **Point of View** Write a paragraph about "The Great Plains." Review Chapter 3. Tell how the author uses reasons and evidence to support the position that bison should be brought back to the Great Plains.

_____

_____

_____

_____

_____

_____

_____

_____

_____

_____

Topic Sentence

☐ Include the title of the text you read.

☐ Tell whether the author uses reasons and evidence to support his position.

☐ Include the author's position.

Evidence

☐ Include reasons the author gives.

☐ Include facts the author uses as evidence.

☐ Restate details and facts from the text correctly.

Concluding Statement

☐ Restate how the author uses reasons and evidence to support his position.

Linked In

Big Idea
How are we all connected?

Talk About It

Weekly Concept Joining Forces

Essential Question

How do different groups contribute to a cause?

Go Digital!

COLLABORATE Write words to describe how each group in the photograph is contributing to a cause.

Contributing to a Cause

 Describe a time when you worked with others for a cause. Use some words you wrote above.

©Craig Lovell/Corbis

Vocabulary

 Work with a partner to complete each activity.

1 survival

List two things a plant needs for *survival*.

_____

_____

2 intercept

Describe what happens when a player *intercepts* a ball.

3 contributions

What *contributions* can people make to help an animal shelter? Give two examples.

_____

_____

4 operations

List two computer *operations* you can do.

_____

_____

5 diversity

Circle words and phrases that are synonyms for *diversity*.

variety   many kinds   sameness

6 recruits

Who would you ask to be *recruits* for a soccer team? Name two people. Explain your choices.

_____

_____

_____

7 enlisted

What would you do to get people to *enlist* for a clean-up project in the community?

_____

_____

8 **bulletin**

Draw a *bulletin* about a school carnival. Use pictures and words.

High-Utility Words

▶ Indefinite Pronouns

A pronoun takes the place of a noun. Some pronouns are indefinite, or do not refer to specific people, places, or things. *No one, someone,* and *everyone* are examples of indefinite pronouns.

Circle the indefinite pronouns.

My cat Whiskers wasn't in my bedroom where she usually naps. So (everyone) started looking for her. Someone thought she might be hiding under the bed. Others thought she might have wandered downstairs. But no one could find her anywhere. Then we heard something in the kitchen. We found her eating at her dish!

My Notes

Use this page to take notes during your first read of "Shipped Out."

_____

_____

_____

_____

_____

_____

_____

_____

_____

_____

_____

SHIPPED OUT

Essential Question

How do different groups contribute to a cause?

Read about how a young girl learns how to contribute to the war effort during World War II.

My name is Libby Kendall, and some days I feel like I am a prisoner of war. I'm trapped, not able to do much while the war goes on. Like my dad, I've packed my things and shipped out, away from home. Unlike my dad, however, nothing I do will help the Allies win World War II.

My dad went to work as a mechanic on a battleship in the Pacific Ocean. I'm stuck in my aunt's apartment above her bakery. Mom says it's just for a few months while she works double shifts at the clothing factory. Mom makes uniforms. I asked her if she snuck things like poems for the soldiers into the pockets. She said the pockets were to hold tools for war **survival**, not silly things like poetry.

No one appreciates my creative **contributions** to the war effort, but Aunt Lucia says my help is important, since both her workers joined the army.

On my first day, Aunt Lucia explained the bakery **operations**. First, we get up early to prepare the dough. Next, we bake breads and muffins. Then I help customers while Aunt Lucia makes cakes and cookies for the afternoon. Whenever the phone rings, she races to **intercept** the call. She's always worried that it might be bad news, so she wants to be the first to hear it.

After dinner, Aunt Lucia invites neighbors to listen to the radio. Some are immigrants from a wide **diversity** of backgrounds. Lucia and others help **translate** the news into several languages. I listen for any **bulletin** about fighting in the Pacific.

Sean Qualls

Text Evidence

1 Organization Ⓐ Ⓒ Ⓣ

Draw a box around the detail that tells where Libby is living. List two events that led Libby to move there.

_____

_____

_____

_____

2 Comprehension
Theme

Reread the page. **Underline** details that show what Libby and her family think about her contributions to the war effort.

3 Expand Vocabulary

To **translate** is to change words into a different language. **Circle** clues to the meaning of _translate_. What does Aunt Lucia _translate_?

_____

① Organization ACT

Draw a box around paragraphs that describe events that happened in the past. What words tell you Libby is remembering events?

_____

② Expand Vocabulary

A person who is **ashamed** feels sorry or embarrassed. **Circle** clues to the meaning of *ashamed*.

③ Comprehension

Theme

Underline text that tells how Libby feels when her dad says he is joining the navy. How does Libby feel now? What does she learn?

_____

_____

_____

I remember how closely my parents followed news about the war, which I rarely understood. They often whispered to one another. I'd say, "Speak up! I can't hear you!" They'd frown and leave me alone to talk in private.

One night, they came into the living room and turned off the radio. At first I was angry, but they had serious looks on their faces. "Our country's at war," Dad said. "The military will be looking for new **recruits**. I know about ships and engines, so I am going to join the navy."

"You can't just leave," I said. I stomped on the floor for emphasis and stormed off to my bedroom. Looking back, I feel **ashamed.** I wished I hadn't acted so selfishly. The military needed Dad's help.

This morning, Aunt Lucia can tell I'm feeling down. She asks me to help her decorate cupcakes for a fundraiser tonight. At first I'm not interested. Then I realize I can make flags with the frosting and berries. I make red stripes from strawberries and a patch of blue from blueberries. Soon I have a whole tray of cupcakes decorated like flags.

Sean Qualls

"Wonderful!" Aunt Lucia says. "I'm sure they'll sell better than anything else!"

At last, I feel like I've done something right. I think of the money we might make and how it may buy **supplies** my dad needs.

"I **enlisted** in the navy to help restore democracy in the world," my dad said on the day he left. "Now you be a good navy daughter and sail straight." I promised I would. As he left, I slipped a poem into his coat pocket. "Here's a little rhyme to pass the day," it said. "I love you back in the U.S.A.!"

I wish I could send a cupcake to my dad. Instead, I'll draw a plate of cupcakes piled high and send the picture off to the Pacific with a letter. That way, my dad will have plenty to share with everyone there.

Text Evidence

❶ Expand Vocabulary

Supplies are things you need to do work. **Circle** a clue to the meaning of *supplies*.

❷ Organization A C T

Draw a box around the paragraph that describes an event that happened in the past. What does this memory cause Libby to do?

_____

_____

❸ Comprehension
Theme

Review what Libby says at the beginning about her contributions to the war effort. **Underline** text that tells how Libby feels about her efforts at the end. What does Libby learn about helping a cause?

_____

_____

335

Respond to Reading

Discuss ▶ Work with a partner. Use the discussion starters to answer the questions below about "Shipped Out." Write the page numbers to show where you found text evidence.

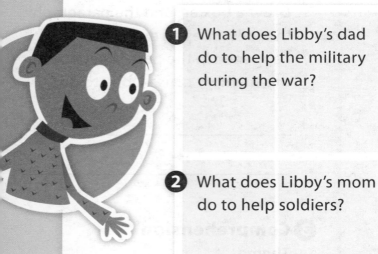

❓ **Questions**	💬 **Discussion Starters**	🔍 **Text Evidence**
1 What does Libby's dad do to help the military during the war?	▶ Libby's dad helps the war effort by… ▶ Libby's dad works as… ▶ I read that Libby's dad wants to help during the war because…	Page(s): _____
2 What does Libby's mom do to help soldiers?	▶ Libby's mom helps soldiers by… ▶ I read that Libby's mom makes… ▶ I know that Libby's mom works extra hard because I read that…	Page(s): _____
3 What does Libby do to help during the war?	▶ Libby helps by… ▶ Another way Libby contributes to the war effort is by… ▶ I read that…	Page(s): _____

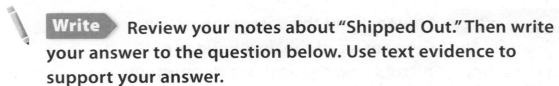

Write Review your notes about "Shipped Out." Then write your answer to the question below. Use text evidence to support your answer.

What do Libby and people in her family do to contribute to the war effort?

_____

_____

_____

_____

_____

_____

_____

_____

_____

_____

Write About Reading

Shared Read

Read an Analysis **Theme** Read the paragraph below about "Shipped Out." Gina analyzed the descriptions of a character's feelings. She told how the author's descriptions conveyed the theme.

Student Model

Topic Sentence

Circle the topic sentence. What is Gina going to write about?

Evidence

Draw a box around the evidence that Gina includes. What other details from "Shipped Out" would you include?

Concluding Statement

Underline the concluding statement. Why is this sentence a good wrap up?

In "Shipped Out," the author's descriptions of Libby's feelings helped to convey a theme. At first, Libby feels trapped. She thinks she can't do anything to help the Allies win the war. Libby also feels ashamed of the way she acted when her dad left. She realizes that the military needed her dad's help. After Libby decorates the cupcakes for the fundraiser, she feels like she did something right. These descriptions help me know that Libby learned a lesson: Everyone has something to contribute.

Leveled Reader

Write an Analysis ▷ **Theme** Write a paragraph about "Mrs. Gleeson's Records." Analyze the author's descriptions of a character's feelings. Tell how they help to convey the theme of the story.

_____

_____

_____

_____

_____

_____

_____

_____

_____

_____

_____

Topic Sentence

☐ Include the title of the text you read.

☐ Tell whether descriptions of a character's feelings helped convey a theme.

Evidence

☐ Describe the character's feelings.

☐ Explain why the character's feelings change.

Concluding Statement

☐ Restate that the author's descriptions of a character's feelings convey a theme.

☐ Include the theme.

Talk About It

Weekly Concept Getting Along

Essential Question

What actions can we take to get along with others?

Go Digital!

Write words to describe ways people can get along with each other.

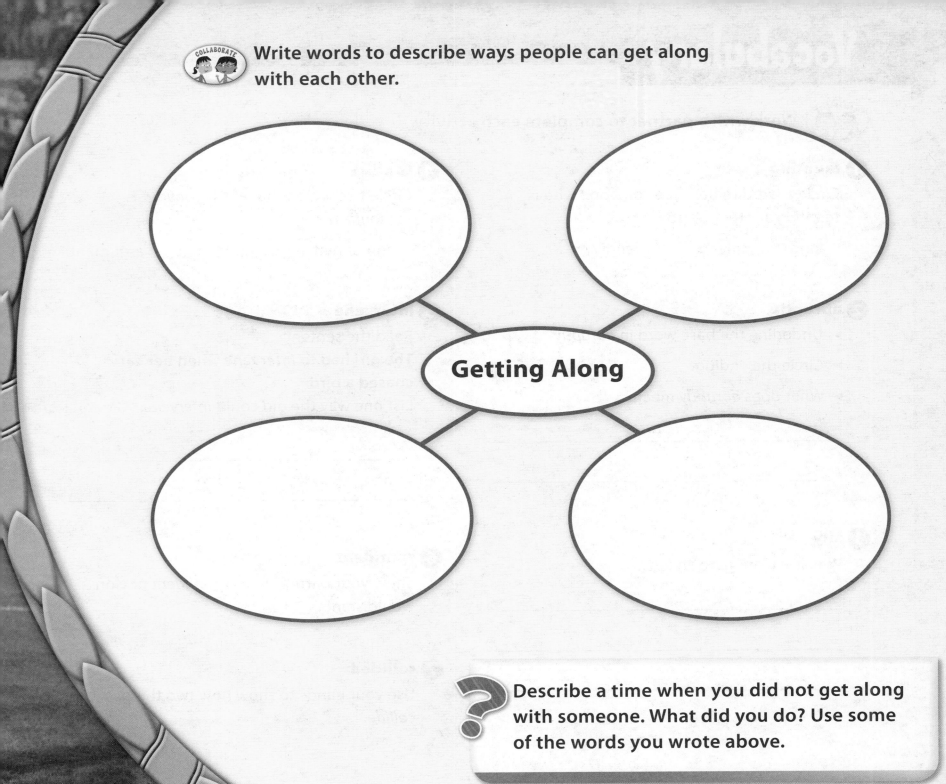

Getting Along

Describe a time when you did not get along with someone. What did you do? Use some of the words you wrote above.

Vocabulary

 Work with a partner to complete each activity.

1 **taunting**

Circle a word to describe someone who is *taunting* another person.

    kind   mean   friendly

2 **abruptly**

▶ Underline the base word in *abruptly*.

▶ Circle the ending.

▶ What does *abruptly* mean?

_____

_____

3 **ally**

Why is a teammate an *ally*?

_____

_____

4 **conflict**

Circle two words that are synonyms for *conflict*.

    agreement   disagreement   argument

5 **intervene**

Read the sentence:
The girl had to *intervene* when her cat chased a bird.
List one way the girl could *intervene*.

_____

_____

6 **confident**

Show your partner how a *confident* person would stand.

7 **collided**

Use your hands to show how two things *collide*.

342

8 **protective**

Think of a job in which a person wears *protective* clothing. Draw a picture of the person at work.

High-Utility Words

▶ **Prefix *un-***

The prefix *un-* means "not." For example, *unhappy* means "not happy."

Circle words with the prefix *un-*.

Friday was an (unusual) day. Joe and Kara were working on a science project. At first, Joe was unhappy because he thought Kara was unfriendly. But when Joe and Kara started the project, something unexpected happened. Kara was helpful and nice. Joe was unsure what caused the change, but he was glad they were getting along.

My Notes

Use this page to take notes during your first read of "The Bully."

The Bully

? **Essential Question**

What actions can we take to get along with others?

Read about how one student tries to deal with a bully.

Michael saw trouble coming from the end of the school hallway. Standing by the stairs was J.T., the school bully. He seemed to enjoy **taunting** anyone he felt like. He was tall and strong, so few of his victims stood up to him to defend themselves. Michael hated the idea that he let J.T. get away with bullying others. Yet, like most of the other kids who were picked on, he usually just took it quietly.

J.T. walked toward Michael, his eyes locked on the books that Michael carried. He stopped **abruptly** and snapped at Michael, "Hey, let me see those books!" A group of students watched as Michael held out the books, trying not to tremble and reveal how **nervous** he was.

J.T. grabbed a math book, looked inside, and then shoved it at Michael, who dropped all the books he held. "Hey, those books are school property," J.T. barked, "so don't let them fall to the floor!" Then he walked away, laughing loudly.

Michael, his cheeks turning red, half kicked the fallen books. Suddenly a hand picked up one of the books. "You look like you could use an **ally**," a friendly voice said with a laugh.

Marcelo Baez

❶ Comprehension
Theme

Underline what Michael usually does when J.T. picks on him. What does this tell you about Michael?

_____

_____

_____

❷ Expand Vocabulary

When someone is **nervous**, they are fearful. **Circle** a clue to the meaning of *nervous*.

❸ Connection of Ideas Ⓐ Ⓒ Ⓣ

How does Michael feel after J.T. makes him drop his books? **Draw a box** around text evidence.

_____

_____

_____

345

Text Evidence

① Comprehension
Theme

Draw a box around text that tells what Michael wants Ramon to do. Does Ramon think this is a good or bad idea? What does he do and say that tells you this?

_____

_____

② Connection of Ideas

Circle Ramon's grandmother's saying. **Circle** the meaning. What does Ramon mean when he tells Michael to "Try honey instead"?

_____

_____

_____

③ Expand Vocabulary

Underline a word that is a synonym for **advice**.

346

Michael turned and saw that it was Ramon. He was the school's star baseball player, basketball player, and everything-else-player you could name. Michael couldn't believe he was stopping to help him. The two had barely spoken to each other since the year began.

"Thanks," Michael sighed. "I don't know what his problem is."

"In my opinion," Ramon said, "you need to find a way to end this **conflict** with J.T." Michael nodded, unsure what to say. "Well," Ramon continued, "I can tell you what my grandmother used to tell me whenever I had a problem with someone. She'd say, 'You can catch more flies with honey than with vinegar.'"

Looking puzzled, Michael asked, "What does that mean?"

"It means that being kind to your enemies may work better than being angry at them," Ramon explained.

"What if you just **intervene** and tell J.T. to stop picking on me?" Michael suggested. "I bet he'll leave me alone if you threaten him."

"That's vinegar," Ramon laughed as he walked away. "Try honey instead."

That night, Michael thought about the **advice** Ramon had given him. It sounded like a good plan, but Michael wasn't **confident** that Ramon's suggestion would work.

The next day, when J.T. saw Michael, he walked straight towards him. Michael knew it would be just a matter of seconds before the two of them **collided** in the middle of the hall.

Marcelo Baez

As J.T. came nearer, Michael wished he had Ramon's **protective** arm to stop the bully from attacking. Then, suddenly, the unexpected happened. J.T. accidentally tripped. He fell down, and his own armful of books went flying across the floor.

The crowd of students in the hallway froze, waiting to see what J.T. would do next. As J.T. slowly stood up, Michael had an idea. He bent down and helped J.T. pick up his books.

Michael said, "You look like you could use an ally."

J.T. was speechless at Michael's kindness. He took the books and **muttered** quickly, "Uh, thanks."

As J.T. walked away, Michael saw Ramon, who gave him a big smile and a "thumbs-up." "My grandmother would be proud of you," Ramon said.

"It's just honey," Michael grinned. "I hope it sticks."

Text Evidence

1 Expand Vocabulary

To **mutter** means to speak in a low voice. **Underline** a detail in the text that tells why J.T. *muttered*.

2 Comprehension
Theme

Draw a box around what Michael does after he sees J.T. trip. What does J.T. say and do next? What is the story's message?

_____

_____

_____

3 Connection of Ideas Ⓐ Ⓒ Ⓣ

Circle what Ramon says when he sees Michael. Why does he say this?

_____

_____

_____

Respond to Reading

Discuss Work with a partner. Use the discussion starters to answer the questions below about "The Bully." Write the page numbers where you found text evidence.

 **Questions**

 **Discussion Starters**

Text Evidence

1 What does Michael usually do when J.T. bullies him?

▶ When J.T. bullies him, Michael usually…

▶ I noticed that Michael…

Page(s): _____

2 How does Ramon help Michael solve his problem with J.T.?

▶ Ramon helps Michael solve his problem by…

▶ Ramon tells Michael to…

▶ I know this because I read that…

Page(s): _____

3 What does Michael do at the end of the story to solve his problem with J.T.?

▶ Michael solves his problem with J.T. by…

▶ J.T. acts differently to Michael when…

▶ I read that…

Page(s): _____

Mike Moran

Write Review your notes about "The Bully." Then write your answer to the question below. Use text evidence to support your answer.

What does Michael do to get along with J.T.?

_____

_____

_____

_____

_____

_____

_____

_____

_____

_____

_____

Marcelo Baez

Write About Reading

Shared Read

Genre Read the paragraph below about "The Bully." Carter told his opinion about how the author developed a realistic story.

Student Model

Topic Sentence

Circle the topic sentence. What is Carter going to write about?

Evidence

Draw a box around the evidence that Carter includes. What other details from "The Bully" would you include?

Concluding Statement

Underline the concluding statement. Why is this sentence a good wrap up?

In "The Bully," I think the author did a good job of creating a realistic story. Michael, Ramon, and J.T. are like real kids. Michael is picked on by J.T. He doesn't do anything because J.T. is tall and strong. Real kids have problems like this. Ramon gives Michael advice rather than fighting J.T. Classmates in real life sometimes give advice to each other. At the end of the story, Michael helps J.T. when he accidentally trips. I think this is a realistic way for Michael to solve his problem with J.T.

Leveled Reader

Write an Analysis   **Genre** Write a paragraph about "Winning Friends." Tell your opinion about how the author developed a realistic story.

_____

_____

_____

_____

_____

_____

_____

_____

_____

_____

_____

_____

Topic Sentence

☐ Include the title of the text you read.

☐ Tell whether the author did a good job of creating a realistic story.

Evidence

☐ Describe details about the characters and events that are realistic.

☐ Tell why each character or event is realistic.

Concluding Statement

☐ Restate your opinion about how well the author created a realistic story.

Essential Question

How are living things adapted to their environment?

Go Digital!

352

 Write words to describe the animal you see in the photograph. Tell how it fits in with its environment.

Adaptations

 Tell how the animal is able to hide in the environment. Use words you wrote above.

Vocabulary

 Work with a partner to complete each activity.

1 dormant

Circle an antonym for *dormant*.

active   not active   resting

2 cache

Where would you *cache* your favorite book?

_____

_____

_____

3 hibernate

Which of these things do animals do when they *hibernate*? Circle your answer.

hunt   rest   climb

4 insulates

Which item better *insulates* against the cold?

a blanket   a sheet

5 forage

Describe what squirrels do when they *forage* for food.

_____

_____

_____

6 frigid

Show how you would feel on a *frigid* day. Use your face, hands, and body.

7 adaptation

▶ Underline the base word in *adaptation*.

▶ Circle the suffix.

▶ What does *adaptation* mean?

_____

_____

_____

8 **agile**

Draw a picture of a performer or athlete who must be *agile*.

High-Utility Words

Suffixes *-ion* and *-ation*

The suffixes *-ion* and *-ation* mean "the act or process." *Discussion* means "the act of discussing."

Circle the words that end in *-ion* or *-ation*.

Maria's family put on a (celebration) at the park on Saturday. Mom put up decorations. Dad gave out directions so guests could get to the party. People came by bike, car, and public transportation. The party was a success because the park was a perfect place for relaxation and conversation.

My Notes

Use this page to take notes during your first read of "Mysterious Oceans."

Shared Read Genre • Expository Text

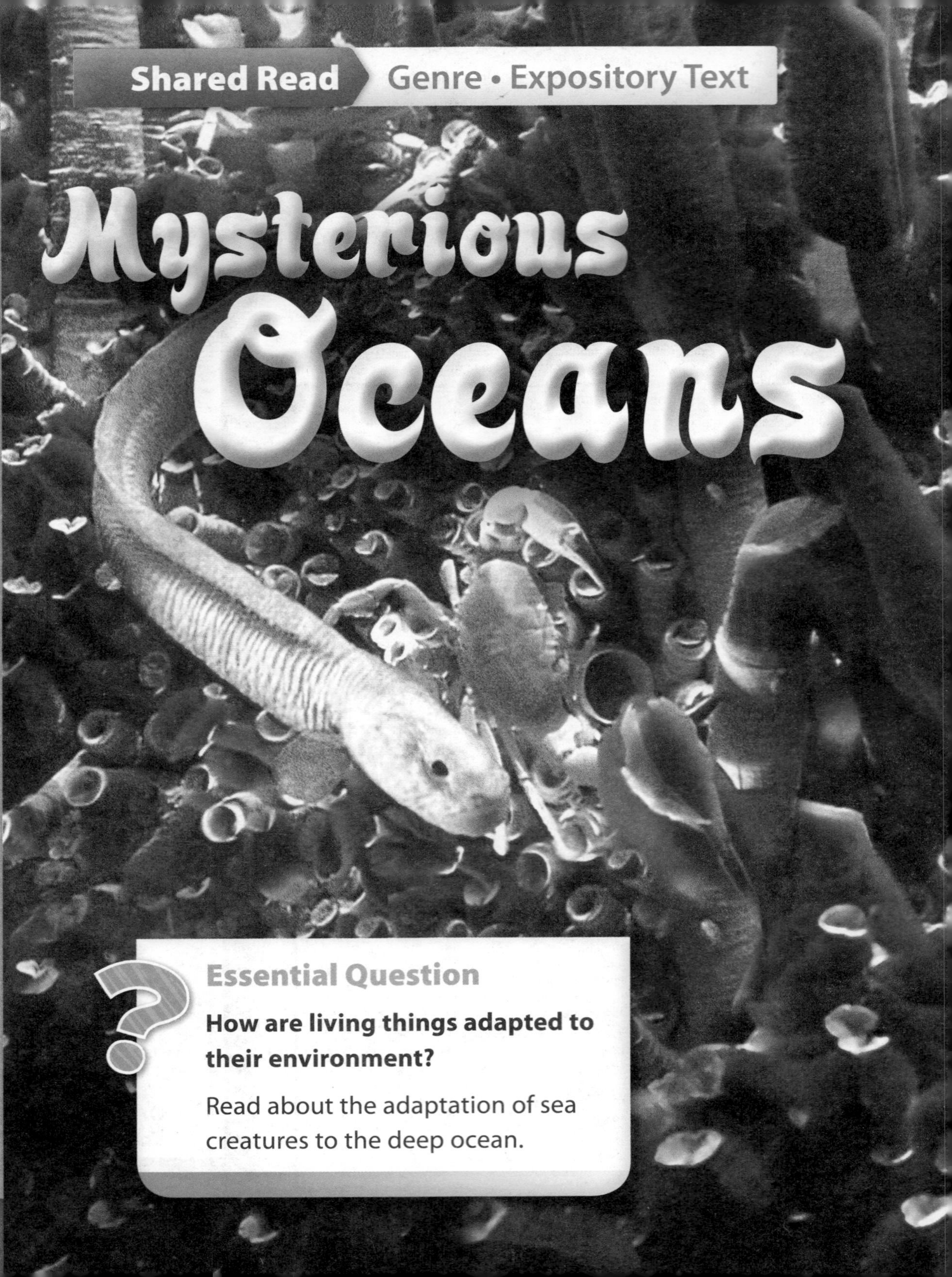

Mysterious Oceans

Essential Question

How are living things adapted to their environment?

Read about the adaptation of sea creatures to the deep ocean.

Deep Diving

In the ocean, there is a creature that has no mouth, eyes, or stomach. Its soft body is enclosed in a white tube and topped with a red plume. It can grow eight feet tall. This giant tube worm lives on the deep, dark ocean floor.

The deep ocean, in contrast to shallow waters, covers almost two-thirds of Earth's surface. On average, oceans are about two miles deep. However, the deepest point on Earth is nearly seven miles down in the Pacific Ocean.

◄ **Some deep ocean fish are swimming among tube worms. New ocean species are being discovered all the time.**

The ocean's floor consists of plains, canyons, and mountains. There are also active, **dormant**, and extinct volcanoes. This undersea world has **frigid**, icy temperatures and little sunlight.

The deep ocean is a **mysterious** environment because much of it has been unexplored. Little is known about the sea creatures that live there. Do some of them **cache** food, storing it as land animals do? Do any creatures **hibernate**? Some species, like the giant squid, have only recently been seen alive. Before that, we knew they existed only because their dead bodies had been found.

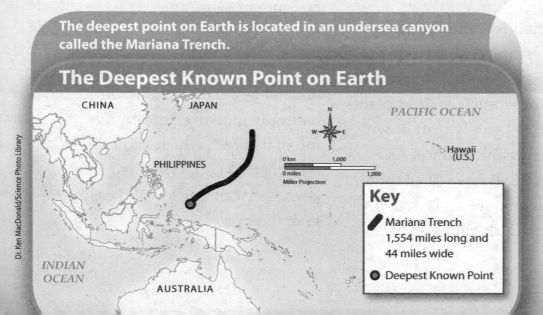

The deepest point on Earth is located in an undersea canyon called the Mariana Trench.

The Deepest Known Point on Earth

CHINA

JAPAN

PACIFIC OCEAN

PHILIPPINES

Hawaii (U.S.)

0 km 1,000
0 miles 1,000
Miller Projection

INDIAN OCEAN

AUSTRALIA

Key

Mariana Trench
1,554 miles long and
44 miles wide

● Deepest Known Point

Dr. Ken MacDonald/Science Photo Library

Text Evidence

❶ Genre A C T
Expository Text

Review the map and key. Point to the deepest known point. Name the country closest to this point.

_____

_____

❷ Expand Vocabulary

Something that is **mysterious** is not well understood. Which words and phrases are clues to the meaning of *mysterious*?

_____

_____

❸ Comprehension
Cause and Effect

Circle causes. **Underline** effects. Why do we know giant squid exist?

_____

_____

357

Text Evidence

1 Genre ⒶⒸⓉ

Expository Text

Draw a box around the caption that describes an adaptation.

2 Comprehension

Cause and Effect

Underline one effect of the invention of the submarine. Why have scientists only seen five percent of the underwater world?

_____

_____

3 Expand Vocabulary

When you **anticipate** something, you predict or expect it. What did scientists *anticipate* about life in the deep ocean? **Circle** text that tells why they *anticipated* this.

_____

_____

A striated frogfish (left) lures its prey. Its nose is an adaptation to life in the deep ocean.

A basket starfish rests in a deep-sea coral reef.

Amazing Adaptations

Once a submersible, or submarine, was invented that could descend farther than any other craft, scientists could then reach the deep ocean floor. However, exploration has been difficult, so they have seen only five percent of the underwater world.

As scientists **anticipated**, few sea creatures survive in the deep ocean. Scientists knew that food sources, such as dead plants and animals, rarely drift down from the ocean's surface. As a result, animals have to adapt to an environment that is not only frigid and dark but also has little food.

One example of an **adaptation** to this environment is seen in the starfish. Deep-sea starfish grow larger and are more aggressive, or forceful, than shallow-water starfish. They don't wait for a snail to pass by. They actively **forage** for food. They reach up their five arms, which have pincers at the ends, to catch **agile**, fast-moving shrimp.

Anglerfish also are adapted to finding scarce food. This type of fish has a bioluminous, or naturally glowing, lure on the top of its head, which allows it to attract other fish. With their huge jaws, they can quickly and easily grab their prey.

Heated Habitats

What has surprised scientists, however, is the discovery of another type of environment on the deep ocean floor. They found that cracks, or vents, in Earth's surface exist underwater, just as they do on dry land. Sea water rushes into these vents, where it mixes with chemicals. The water is also heated by magma, or hot melted rock. When the water from the vent **bursts**, or gushes, back into the ocean, it creates geysers and hot springs.

Mussels, worms, and spider crabs live near heated vents in the ocean floor.

Scientists found that areas around these vents are habitats for many species, including tube worms, huge clams, eyeless shrimp, crabs, mussels, and bacteria. One odd creature, the Pompeii worm, has a coat of bacteria on its back. As far as scientists can determine, this coat **insulates** it from heat.

How can so much life exist where there is so little food? Many creatures transform the chemicals from the vents into food. The process is called chemosynthesis. Because of chemosynthesis, animals are able to flourish in these habitats. Those that don't use chemosynthesis for food, such as crabs, eat the ones that do.

There are many mysteries to be found and solved at the bottom of the deep sea. In the last few decades alone, scientists have discovered more than 1,500 ocean species! If scientists keep exploring, they are sure to discover many more.

Text Evidence

1 Expand Vocabulary

When something **bursts**, it pushes forward or out. **Circle** a synonym for *bursts*.

2 Genre A C T
Expository Text

Draw a box around a heading on this page. Which habitat in the text does the heading refer to?

_____

_____

3 Comprehension
Cause and Effect

Reread the page. **Circle** each cause. **Underline** each effect. Why are animals able to flourish near vents?

_____

_____

Respond to Reading

 Discuss Work with a partner. Use the discussion starters to answer the questions below about "Mysterious Oceans." Write the page numbers where you found text evidence.

 Questions

Discussion Starters

Text Evidence

1 How is a deep-sea starfish different from a starfish that lives in shallow water?	▸ Deep-sea starfish get their food by… ▸ Starfish that live in shallow water are not as… ▸ Compared to other starfish, deep-sea starfish are…	Page(s): _____
2 How do anglerfish get food in the deep ocean?	▸ Anglerfish get food by… ▸ Anglerfish can grab prey with… ▸ I read that…	Page(s): _____
3 How do creatures that live near ocean vents get food?	▸ Many creatures that live near vents get their food by… ▸ Other creatures get their food by… ▸ I know this because I read that…	Page(s): _____

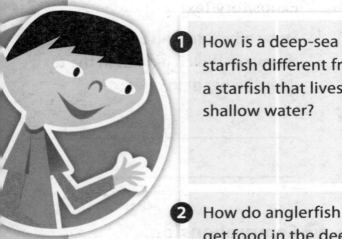

Write Review your notes about "Mysterious Oceans." Then write your answer to the question below. Use text evidence to support your answer.

How are some sea creatures adapted to living in the deep ocean?

_____

_____

_____

_____

_____

_____

_____

_____

_____

_____

Write About Reading

Shared Read

Student Model

I think the author of "Mysterious Oceans" did a good job of using causes and effects to explain why some animals are adapted to the deep ocean environment. Because little food drifts down to the deep ocean, deep-sea starfish are aggressive. They go after the food they eat. Anglerfish have a lure on top of their heads that attracts prey. Many creatures get their food from chemicals. I think all of these effects explain why some animals are adapted to living in a deep ocean environment.

Topic Sentence

Circle the topic sentence. What is Ali going to write about?

Evidence

Draw a box around the evidence that Ali includes. What other information from "Mysterious Oceans" would you include?

Concluding Statement

Underline the concluding statement. Why is this sentence a good wrap up?

Leveled Reader

Cause and Effect Write a paragraph about "Cave Creatures." Review Chapter 1. Tell your opinion about how the author uses cause-and-effect relationships to explain the topic.

_____
_____
_____
_____
_____
_____
_____
_____
_____
_____
_____

Topic Sentence

☐ Include the title of the text you read.

☐ Tell your opinion about how the author uses cause-and-effect relationships to explain a topic.

☐ Include the topic

Evidence

☐ Give examples of cause-and-effect relationships that explain the topic.

☐ Restate details from the text correctly.

Concluding Statement

☐ Restate your opinion about how the author uses cause-and-effect relationships to explain a topic.

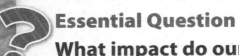

Essential Question

What impact do our actions have on our world?

Go Digital!

Write words to describe what the people in the photograph are doing. Tell how their actions will make a difference.

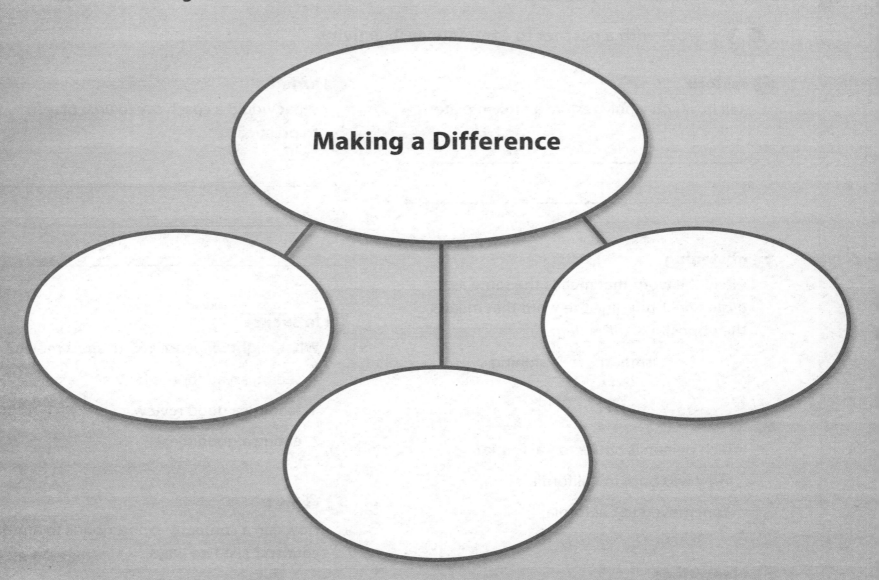

Making a Difference

 Describe a time when you caused a change in the world around you. Use some of the words above.

Vocabulary

 Work with a partner to complete each activity.

1 restore

Tell how you would *restore* a broken plate.

_____

_____

2 glistening

Circle the word that means the same as *glistening*. Underline the word that means the opposite of *glistening*.

dull   smooth   shining

3 native

Which person is *native* to California?

Amy was born in California.

Tom moved to California.

4 plantations

Underline items that might come from *plantations*.

banana   fish   cotton

5 urged

What would a coach say to *urge* players to practice?

_____

_____

_____

6 influence

What might *influence* you to see a movie?

seeing an ad for the movie

reading a good review

eating a good meal

7 export

How can a company *export* goods to another country? List two ways.

_____

_____

8 **landscape**

Draw a picture of the *landscape* of your region. Label any major landforms.

High-Utility Words

▶ **Suffix -*ment***

The suffix -*ment* means the "act of" or "state of." For example, *movement* means "the act of moving."

Circle words that end in -*ment*.

Mr. Lee was an important community leader. His work made an (improvement) on the town. His greatest accomplishment was saving the old train station. He saw that it needed repairs. He made an arrangement with the mayor to fix it. He got community involvement, too. People donated their time and money. Soon, the station was restored. This was an achievement!

My Notes

Use this page to take notes during your first read of "Words to Save the World."

_____

_____

_____

_____

_____

_____

_____

_____

_____

_____

_____

_____

_____

Words to Save the World

The Work of Rachel Carson

Essential Question

What impact do our actions have on our world?

Read about how the biologist Rachel Carson used the power of writing to change the world.

Combining her love of nature with a belief in scientific accuracy, the writer Rachel Carson raised awareness about environmental problems. As a result, the U.S. government passed laws to protect the environment. Many people believe it was Rachel's book *Silent Spring* that started the environmental movement that continues today.

Early Influences

Rachel was born in Springdale, Pennsylvania, in 1907. During her childhood, her mother **encouraged** her to explore the **landscape** around the family's farm. Rachel's love of nature grew and affected her decisions throughout her life. For example, she first wanted to study writing. However, she later chose to study biology. As she studied ocean animals,

◀ **Rachel preferred working alone as she gathered information.**

the **glistening** and shimmering seascape captured her interest.

From an early age, Rachel also loved to write. Her writing skills were useful in her career. She began by creating radio programs for the U.S. Bureau of Fisheries. She then became an editor for the agency. She also wrote her own articles about nature for newspapers and magazines. Rachel published three books about the ocean and its **native** plants and animals: *Under the Sea-Wind*, *The Sea Around Us*, and *The Edge of the Sea*.

Rachel supported the ideas in her writing with well-researched facts.

(l) Alfred Eisenstaedt/Time Life Pictures/Getty Images; (r) Alfred Eisenstaedt/Time & Life Pictures/Getty Images

Text Evidence

❶ Comprehension
Problem and Solution

What kinds of problems did Rachel raise awareness about? **Underline** what the government did to try to solve these problems.

_____

_____

❷ Expand Vocabulary

To **encourage** means to urge to do something. What did Rachel's mother *encourage* her to do?

_____

_____

❸ Connection of Ideas

Circle the subjects Rachel was interested in as a child. **Draw a box** around the paragraph that tells about her career. What was Rachel interested in as a child and as an adult?

_____

_____

369

Text Evidence

1 Comprehension
Problem and Solution

Underline the sentence that describes the Huckins's problem. What caused the problem?

_____

_____

_____

2 Comprehension
Problem and Solution

Circle steps Rachel took to solve the Huckins's problem.

3 Connection of Ideas (ACT)

Draw a box around the detail that tells what Rachel urged readers of *Silent Spring* to imagine. List one effect this had on readers.

_____

_____

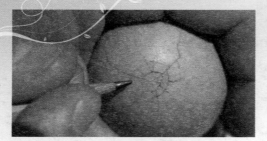

Rachel's research revealed that DDT caused damage to birds and eggs.

A Call to Action

One day, Rachel got a letter from friends, Olga and Stuart Huckins. They described problems resulting from the spraying of the chemical DDT on private land reserved for wildlife. Chemical companies had created DDT as a way to stop crop-eating insects on farms and **plantations**. On the Huckins's land, however, DDT also seemed to harm birds.

In response, Rachel hired people to study the Huckins's claim. When she realized the study was taking a long time, she became worried. She decided to study the problem alone and publish her findings. She wanted to warn people about the dangers of these

chemicals. To emphasize the issue, she **urged** readers to imagine a world without songbirds. The book's title, *Silent Spring*, describes this possible effect of pesticide misuse.

Rachel's book encouraged readers to speak out against the chemical companies. Readers demanded an investigation. They asked the government to control pesticide use. In response, President John Kennedy created a Congressional committee to study the problem. Rachel spoke at the committee's meetings and gave facts to **influence** its decisions.

Food chains show how pesticides intended for insects can affect animals.

Sample Food Chains

LEVEL IN FOOD CHAIN	LAND FOOD CHAIN	OCEAN FOOD CHAIN
Producer	grass	phytoplankton
Consumer	grasshopper	zooplankton
Consumer	rat	fish
Consumer	snake	seal

A Strong Reaction

Meanwhile, chemical companies tried to speak out against Rachel's claims. They published reports that put down her ideas. They made television advertisements that told people that their products were safe. But they could not change many people's opinions about pesticide use.

Rachel worried that once pesticides poisoned an area, it might be impossible to **restore** it back to the way it had been before. "Man's attitude toward nature is today critically important simply because we have now acquired a fateful power to **alter** and destroy nature," she said. Her words and her efforts led the United States government to control the use of some pesticides. Even so, chemical companies produced them for **export** to other countries.

Rachel Carson died shortly after *Silent Spring* was published, but her voice survives within her books, expressing her desire to preserve and protect the natural world.

Rachel Carson understood the power her words had to educate others, especially children.

Text Evidence

1 Connection of Ideas Ⓐ Ⓒ Ⓣ

How did Rachel's claims affect chemical companies? **Circle** two effects. How did these actions affect people's opinions?

_____

_____

2 Expand Vocabulary

To **alter** means to change something. **Draw a box** around one way pesticides can *alter* nature.

3 Comprehension
Problem and Solution

Underline the detail that tells Rachel's problem with pesticides. How did Rachel's words and efforts help solve the problem?

_____

_____

_____

Respond to Reading

Discuss Work with a partner. Use the discussion starters to answer the questions below about "Words to Save the World." Write the page numbers where you found text evidence.

 **Questions**   **Discussion Starters**    **Text Evidence**

1 What did Rachel do when she learned about the Huckins's problem with pesticide?

▶ After Rachel learned about the Huckins's problem, she…

▶ To let people know about problems with pesticides, Rachel…

▶ I noticed that Rachel…

Page(s): _____

2 What effect did *Silent Spring* have on readers' opinions of pesticides?

▶ After *Silent Spring* was published, readers…

▶ Another thing readers did was…

▶ I know this because I read that…

Page(s): _____

3 How did Rachel's words affect the government's actions on pesticide use?

▶ Because of Rachel's book, President John Kennedy…

▶ I read that Rachel's words and efforts led the government to…

Page(s): _____

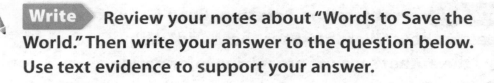

Write ▸ Review your notes about "Words to Save the World." Then write your answer to the question below. Use text evidence to support your answer.

What effect did Rachel's words have on the use of pesticides?

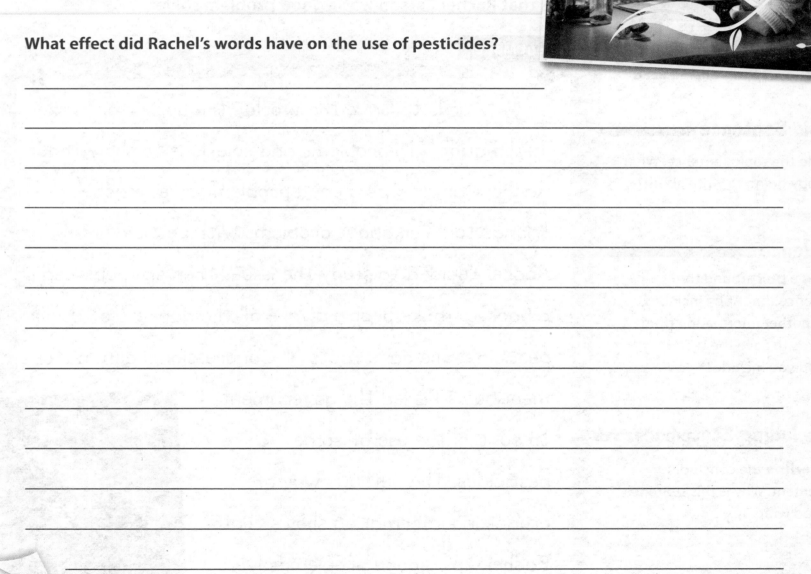

Write About Reading

Shared Read

Student Model

Topic Sentence

Circle the topic sentence. What is Abby going to write about?

Evidence

Draw a box around the evidence that Abby includes. What other information from "Words to Save the World" would you include?

Concluding Statement

Underline the concluding statement. Why is this sentence a good wrap up?

In "Words to Save the World," the author organizes information into problems and solutions to show that Rachel Carson was a good problem solver. Rachel's friends told her about problems with pesticides. Rachel decided to study the issue. Then she published a book to make people aware of the dangers of using pesticide. She gave facts at Congressional committee meetings. This led the government to control the use of some pesticides. The author's way of organizing information shows that Rachel was a good problem solver.

374

Leveled Reader

_____

_____

_____

_____

_____

_____

_____

_____

_____

_____

_____

Topic Sentence

☐ Include the title of the text.

☐ Tell whether the author's organization of information showed that Marjorie was a good problem solver.

Evidence

☐ Include steps that Marjorie took to solve problems.

☐ Include only those steps that show she was a good problem solver. Restate information from the text correctly.

Concluding Statement

☐ Restate how the author showed that Marjorie was a good problem solver.

Talk About It

Weekly Concept Out in the World

Essential Question
What can our connections to the world teach us?

Go Digital!

Write words to describe how people can connect with others and the world around them. Tell what people can learn from these connections.

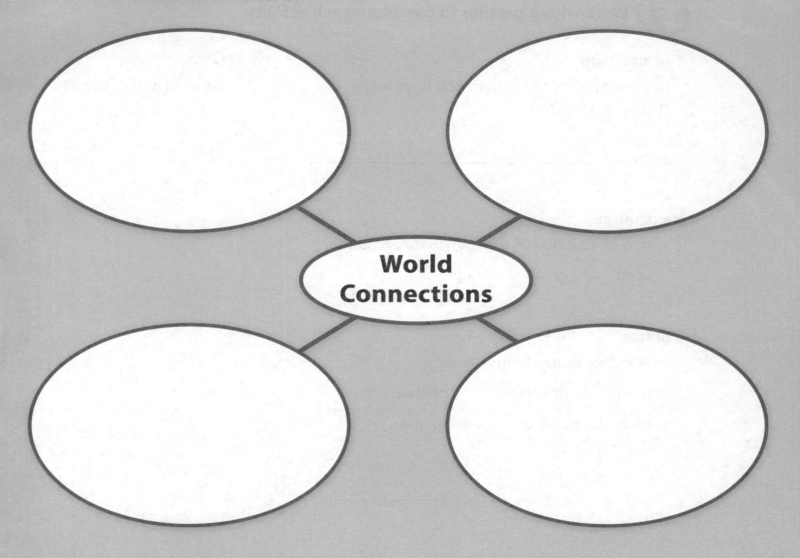

World Connections

 Tell about a connection you have made with a person, place, or thing. Use some words you wrote above.

Vocabulary

 Work with a partner to complete each activity.

1 connection

Name a person with whom you have a strong *connection*.

_____

2 exchange

Which word below is a synonym for *exchange*?

keep   give   trade

3 blares

▶ Which of these things blares?

siren   fire alarm   breeze

▶ Write the name of something else that *blares*.

_____

4 errand

Draw a picture of someone doing an *errand*.

Read the poem. Work with a partner to complete each activity.

The Letter

One gray day,

the rain came pouring down.

Drops of silver

bounced and danced on the sidewalk

on my way home.

An envelope was waiting for me at home.

My name written in neat, careful letters

on its bright face.

I tore it open,

and out poured a stream of sand.

It was a note from Grandpa,

written from a far-off, sunny beach.

And even though the cold rain

still clung to me,

my heart was warm.

5 **personification**

Poets use *personification to* make an object, animal, or idea seem like a person. **Circle** one example of *personification* in "The Letter."

6 **assonance**

Assonance is two or more words with the same vowel sound, such as *stone* and *boat*. Write a pair of words that is an example of *assonance*.

_____

_____

7 **consonance**

Consonance is two or more words with the same middle or final consonant sound, such as *pushed* and *crushed*. **Underline** a pair of words that is an example of *consonance*.

8 **imagery**

Imagery is a description that creates a strong picture. Reread the last five lines. **Draw a box** around one example of *imagery*.

379

My Notes

Use this page to take notes during your first read of "To Travel!" and "Wild Blossoms."

_____

_____

_____

_____

_____

_____

_____

_____

_____

_____

_____

To Travel!

To travel! To travel!
To visit distant places;
To leave my corner of the world
To seek new names and faces.
Adventure! Adventure!
Exploring foreign lands;
If I can leap across the globe,
My universe expands!

A novel waves her arms to me,
"Come read! Come read!" she cries.
Her pages dance with ancient tales,
A feast for hungry eyes!
The paintings on museum walls
Are begging me to tour:
"Leave your home and live our scenes,
A grand exchange for sure!"

To travel! To travel!
Through timeless books and art,
I enter and experience
A life so far apart.

? Essential Question

What can our connections to the world teach us?

Read two poems about connecting with other cultures and with nature.

I sail across the seven seas,
My heart soars like a bird.
And soon I'm hearing languages
I've never, ever heard.

Far across the seven seas,
Aromas fill the air.
Foods I've never, ever tried
Are eaten everywhere!
Music blares a different tune,
And strange, new clothes are worn.
Parents pass on customs
To the young ones who are born.

I've traveled! I've traveled!
It's left me more aware;
A valuable connection
To the universe we share.
By reading books and viewing art,
I've learned a thing or two:
The world was made not just for me,
But made for me and you!

— Jad Abbas

Text Evidence

1 Genre (A)(C)(T)
Poetry

Reread the first stanza on page 380. **Circle** each line that shows a strong feeling. What feeling does the speaker express?

_____

2 Literary Elements
Personification

Reread the second stanza on page 380. **Underline** one example of *personification*.

3 Comprehension
Point of View

Draw a box around details that describe new experiences. What is the speaker's point of view about learning new things?

_____

_____

_____

1 Literary Elements

Assonance

Reread the first three lines aloud. **Underline** an example of *assonance*.

2 Genre A C T

Poetry

A narrative poem tells a story. **Circle** what the speaker of the poem does first. What important event happens next?

_____

_____

3 Comprehension

Point of View

Draw a box around the description of what Grandmother does with the seeds. What does the speaker think about Grandmother's actions?

_____

_____

Wild Blossoms

One bright summer morning, my grandmother asked me to help her plant some flowers. I pedaled my bike downtown, wheels weaving between sunbeams. In the sky, clouds exchanged greetings, their language inaudible, while I, on my errand, brought a long list of seeds to the store. Back on my bike, I followed the same sensible route I always took to Grandmother's house. I watched with surprise as she tore off the tops of the seed packets and shook them willy-nilly around the backyard, then told me to do the same.

"I thought we were planting a garden," I told her,
"with row after row of flowers." She said, "Oh, no!
I prefer a mountain meadow, one with plenty
of variety." As she talked, bees buzzed about
in excitable flight, impatient for blossoms.
Quick swifts and happy sparrows dipped, dove, and darted
after the falling seeds. My grandmother and I
danced about the backyard, arms outstretched, letting seeds
loose on the wind, joyfully dreaming of the wild
beauty that would fill the yard, and us, all summer.

—Amelia Campos

❶ Literary Elements
Consonance

Reread the fourth line aloud. **Circle** an example of *consonance*.

❷ Genre
Poetry

Draw a box around imagery that helps you picture the swifts and sparrows. In your own words, tell what they are doing.

_____

_____

❸ Comprehension
Point of View

Underline words that describe the speaker's and Grandmother's actions. How do you think the speaker feels about planting seeds with Grandmother?

_____

_____

Respond to Reading

Discuss Work with a partner. Use the discussion starters to answer the questions about "To Travel!" and "Wild Blossoms." Write the page numbers where you found text evidence.

 **? Questions**	**Discussion Starters**	**Text Evidence**
1 What does the speaker of "To Travel!" learn about other people through books and art?	▶ One thing the speaker learns about other people is that… ▶ Another thing the speaker learns about other people is that… ▶ I read that…	Page(s): _____
2 What does the speaker of "To Travel!" learn about himself through books and art?	▶ The speaker learns that he is… ▶ The speaker learns that he shares… ▶ I know this because I read that…	Page(s): _____
3 What does the speaker of "Wild Blossoms" learn by helping her grandmother?	▶ One thing the speaker learns from her grandmother is to… ▶ Another thing the speaker learns is how to be… ▶ I noticed that…	Page(s): _____

Mike Moran

Write Review your notes about the poems "To Travel!" and "Wild Blossoms." Then write your answer to the question below. Use text evidence to support your answer.

What does the speaker of each poem learn by connecting to people and places?

_____

_____

_____

_____

_____

_____

_____

_____

_____

_____

Write About Reading

Shared Read

Topic Sentence

Circle the topic sentence. What is Max going to write about?

Evidence

Draw a box around the evidence that Max includes. What other details from "Wild Blossoms" would you include?

Concluding Statement

Underline the concluding statement. Why is this sentence a good wrap up?

Student Model

In "Wild Blossoms," I think the poet did a good job of creating strong imagery. The words "wheels weaving between sunbeams" help me picture the speaker slowly moving the bike on a sunny day. The words "dipped, dove, and darted" and "excitable flight" help me imagine fast-moving birds. The words "arms outstretched" also create strong imagery. I can picture the speaker and Grandmother as they dance. I think all of these details create strong imagery.